How to
Self-Publish
a
Children's Paperback
Picture Book
using
Amazon
Kindle Direct Publishing (KDP)

An Informative Step-by-Step Guide
for Beginners
on Creating and Publishing Their Own Book

www.AbridgeClub.com

Other titles by this author:
Fruits and Veggies Row by Row: Children in the Garden | English
Frutas y Vegetales Fila por Fila: Los Niños en el Jardín | Spanish with English Translation
I Spy with My Little Eye: Vegetables, an Early STEM Experience | English
Espío con Mis Ojitos: Vegetales, Una Experiencia Temprana de STEM | Spanish and English
I Spy with My Little Eye: Fruit, an Early STEM Experience | English
Espío con Mis Ojitos: Fruta una Experiencia Temprana de STEM | Spanish and English
We Eat Food That's Fresh (with downloadable companion song) | English
Comemos Comida Fresca | Spanish and English
Fruits & Veggies Making Faces | English
We Love the Company, A Book About Table Manners | English
Nos Encanta la Compañía: Una Historia Sobre Modales en la Mesa | Spanish and English
When You Find Colors and Shapes | English
Cuando Encuentres los Colores y las Formas | Spanish and English
Quand Vous Trouvez les Couleurs et les Formes | French and English

About the Author:
Angela Russ-Ayon resides in Long Beach, California, with her family.
She is a keynote speaker and trainer on the subject of early childhood development,
and owner of the Russ InVision Company record label, which boasts over
1.5 million in sales, has been presented 9 early childhood music awards
of excellence, and whose music is represented by school suppliers nationwide.
Her specialty is engaging young children in interactive song and dance using fine and gross motor
activities that promote imaginative play, bridge educational gaps, and help build brain pathways.

Primary Illustrator: José Gascón H.

ISBN-13: 978-1-958627-88-4

IngramSpark
2nd Edition

©2019 Russ InVision Company

For information about permission to reproduce selections of this book, contact:

Russ InVision

Russ InVision Company
3219 Conquista Ave., Long Beach, CA 90808
E-mail: info@abridgeclub.com
www.abridgeclub.com
Author: Angela Russ-Ayon

Author's NOTE

Thank you for your time and interest in my book. It is designed to be a basic overview of how to self-publish a children's picture book on Amazon Kindle Direct Publishing (KDP) that you can hold in your hands, rather than a digitized e-book. Did I leave some things out? Absolutely. I touched on aspects of publishing that would typically take many more pages to explain. If you have a question about a topic, I encourage you to broaden your knowledge base with supplemental research. There are some excellent articles, videos, and books that delve deeper into writing, illustrating, and publishing to help you improve your skills.

The first thing you have to do is open an account on Amazon KDP. This includes entering payment, banking, and tax information. Opening a KDP account also opens an Amazon.com account using the same login information. **You are not allowed to open more than one account with KDP** using the same social security number or EIN (Business Tax ID Number). To do so will result in Amazon closing your account, removing your books from their platform, and banning you for life.

Expect links and tips to change as Amazon KDP continues to update its requirements. I will certainly try to keep up. Feel free to contact me directly to schedule an author visit or workshop.

Amazon is not the only place where you can self-publish and distribute your book. The key is to educate yourself about the various options available.

I welcome your constructive criticism, comments, observations, and questions.

Don't forget to have fun. I can't wait to read your book!

- Angela

www.AbridgeClub.com

TABLE of CONTENTS

The PICTURE BOOK

Picture books come in all shapes and sizes and can be for any age. They are specially designed to help young children develop their reading skills. So the books have basic vocabulary that is easily understood and share common characteristics:

- pictures (illustration) with storytelling qualities
- pictures represent but do not mirror the text
- a limited number of words
- lyrical language with a pleasing rhythm
- often contain perfect rhymes
- larger than average print
- usually 32 pages
- a size that will fit on a standard bookshelf, though some are published as BIG books.

Some picture books are **textless** with no words at all. Children gather information from the illustrations and interpret the story solely by inferring and using reasoning skills. As they notice more details, their interpretation of the story changes. The great thing about textless books is that they can be enjoyed by people who can't read and those who speak any language. The problem with textless books is that you have to have the talent to illustrate them.

The Picture Book
AUDIENCE

Most picture books are published for an audience of young readers who are in preschool through first grade, but all ages enjoy them.

Children from newborns to five-year-olds depend on pictures in books to understand a story. In these cases, adults do all of the reading and explain any difficult words or concepts.

First, second, and third graders who can read for themselves still read picture books, but their books typically have more words, and the illustration is downsized to make room for more text. Their books can have as many as 45 pages or more.

The term "children" is very broad. Decide who your audience will be because you can't write for everyone. Choose a specific age group and get to know those children very well.

- Read the bestsellers they read. Discover what interests and entertains Read online reviews for popular children's books.
- Volunteer to read in schools and libraries to see how children respond to different books.
- Study the elements of each story by writing them on story maps. them.

SELF-PUBLISHING

When **self-publishing** a book, authors do all of the work without any help from an established, professional traditional publishing house. Authors handle the entire book publication process with total control and creative freedom. Even though there are specific standards in the industry, no one can tell you what you can and can't do. You set the price of your own book, keeping it reasonable and competitive with similar books in the market. You don't have to sign exclusive contracts, and you can publish very fast, receiving a physical copy of your book as soon as seven to ten days after it goes live on Amazon.com. You can even discount books to negotiate special deals with customers.

Self-publishing a picture book includes:

- Writing your story
- Editing your story
- Illustrating your story
- Laying the text around your illustration
- Designing your cover
- Filing a copyright
- Choosing a publishing and distribution platform (e.g., Amazon KDP, IngramSpark, Lulu, etc.)
- Formatting your book for printing
- Obtaining an ISBN
- Paying for printing
- Selling your book
- Ensuring the quality of your book
- Marketing and promoting yourself and your book

Amazon KDP is a full-service self-publishing print-on-demand (POD) platform that publishes your book for FREE. It offers free online tutorials to help you publish your book on its website. KDP also offers special services for a fee, but you don't have to use them unless you can't figure out how to do something yourself.

Many different **self-publishing companies** are available to authors who want to publish their own books. Some specialize in a few limited services, and others give authors an entire package. But free resources are available to authors willing to do a little research.

PRINTING-ON-DEMAND

Print-on-demand (POD) is a way of digitally printing books only as needed or after they are purchased. The books are printed from a digital file, such as a PDF. On KDP, you can also upload a DOC (.doc), DOCX (.docx), HTML (.html), or RTF (.rtf). Instead of printing a large quantity, like 2,000 copies at a time, POD offers the option of printing as many books as you need.

Authors can order POD books for readings, autograph sessions, book fairs, conventions, or sharing with family and friends for very little investment. POD books allow authors to test the market and see how well their books are received. As a print-on-demand publisher, Amazon Kindle Direct Publishing (KDP) makes books available to markets worldwide without the author or illustrator having to worry about selling, shipping, storage, and distribution, but there are other print-on-demand services out there.

POD books can be made available to buyers quickly, usually within one to two weeks of uploading and approving files. Another benefit of POD is that the book's cover and interior pages can be updated or changed between print runs. To make changes, upload new files, which are reviewed again by Amazon KDP and re-published under the same International Standard Book Number (ISBN).

You cannot, however, change the:

- title and subtitle
- type of binding
- number of pages
- book size
- author's or contributor's name
- language of the book

without changing the ISBN and uploading an entirely new version of the book.

Books with unique features like pop-ups, cut-outs, inserts, page folds, and the like are not a good fit for Amazon KDP. They are considered custom books that require printers with special equipment.

AMAZON
Kindle Direct Publishing (KDP)

Amazon KDP specializes in **print-on-demand (POD),** which means they digitally print books only after the books are ordered by authors or readers.

Amazon KDP publishes books in all specialties: children's books, novels, coloring books, puzzle books, comic books, travel books, cookbooks, magazines, or any combination. And Amazon KDP publishes books in all genres. A **genre** is a particular category of book: science fiction, thriller, horror, comedy, action and adventure, romance, autobiography, and so on.

KDP does not turn authors away because they don't like their stories. They will print almost any book authors submit as long as they have followed their guidelines:

- format the book correctly
- upload the files properly
- publish original work — follow copyright laws
- follow KDP content guidelines

Retail stores all over the world purchase books from Amazon KDP at a discounted price for resale in their online or brick-and-mortar bookstore, like Barnes and Noble or specialty boutique stores.

Limited- or low-content books, such as journals and notebooks, are no longer offered to bookstores and boutiques through Amazon KDP expanded distribution.

There is little, if any, out-of-pocket cost or financial risk to publishing with KDP. Authors manage their books on the KDP **BOOKSHELF** and get paid after selling books. KDP takes a percentage of every book sold based on how much the book costs them to print.

There are many print-on-demand self-publishing services other than KDP that require payment and a signed contract to assist authors in publishing their books. **Authors can publish on KDP without such fee-based services**, but if you feel you will benefit from one, do your homework, interview references, and understand your needs. Read the contract carefully because these services also charge fees to break the contract.

BENEFITS of SELF-PUBLISHING on AMAZON KDP

Here are a few benefits of self-publishing on Amazon KDP.

- Publishing with KDP is FREE.
- Publish quickly. KDP usually reviews and publishes books within 7-10 days or less.
- No contract is required.
- Gain exposure to readers and retailers all around the world.
- See how your book sells over time, and make adjustments as needed.
- Ease of revising the cover, story, or price.
- Set your own retail price, hence your royalty.
- There is no need to print and stock large quantities.
- Authors are paid per book printed regardless of returns.
- KDP deals with the customers and processes all orders.
- Purchase books for resale or drop ship from KDP at a reasonable author's price for giveaways, promotions, signings, book fairs, conventions, and other sales.
- Order any quantity of books.

Authors can order one book or multiple books to sign at a book fair or share with friends and family. If someone wants to buy books directly from an author, an author can place an order on the BOOKSHELF using the PAPERBACK ACTIONS to have any number of books shipped directly from Amazon KDP to the customer at the discounted author's retail price.

For example, authors can buy books from Amazon KDP at an author's cost of say, $3.70, then resell their books at a book fair or book signing for whatever price they want. The price of a book reflects the quality, availability, and popularity of what's inside, not just the cost of printing the book. The time and effort you put into your book are worth something.

Amazon
KDP ROYALTIES

Amazon KDP pays royalties for books sold. A **royalty** is a percentage of money paid to the author and illustrator for books sold. Once Amazon KDP sells books online, it pays authors 60 days after the end of the month in which your books were sold. For example, KDP pays authors royalties at the end of March for books sold from January first through 31st. This is non-negotiable. It does no good to call or email Amazon KDP and ask for your money right after your books are sold, no matter how many were sold.

Don't think you can price your book extremely low, sell thousands with Prime shipping, and get paid royalties. Royalties are not paid on author copies or books priced at a minimum market rate. Minimum pricing, maximum pricing, and royalties can be found on the 3rd page of the KDP BOOKSHELF entitled, "Edit Paperback Rights and Pricing".

There are three ways to get paid for self-publishing books on KDP.

1. Amazon KDP directly deposits royalties in ANY amount into an author's bank account after books are sold.

2. Amazon KDP sends checks to the author when KDP owes the author $100 or more for books sold.

3. Author direct sales: the author orders books online through KDP by paying the discounted author price to KDP. The author directs KDP on where to ship the books, either directly to the customer or directly to the author. The author collects a payment from the customer.

It's important to note that Amazon KDP does not pay <u>advances</u> to authors or illustrators. For information on advances, see *Traditional Publishers.*

AMAZON KDP
RETAIL PRICING

The **retail price** is the total price charged for a book sold to a customer, which includes the cost of printing the book and the money earned from the sale (profit). **Authors set the retail price for their books with KDP**. Shipping is separate. You want your book to be competitively priced with similar books in the market. Pricing is pretty straightforward on KDP, but there are a few limitations, such as the minimum price KDP will allow for the book's size and number of pages and, the calculated royalty authors are paid for each book. When you set up your book in the KDP online BOOKSHELF and enter a retail price on the *Paperback Rights & Pricing* page, KDP calculates what your royalty will be. You can always change the price later.

Do your research. Look at what similar books are selling for in stores and online, and price your book within a reasonable range to give yourself a competitive edge across the globe. In the children's book market, you are also competing with undercutters like Scholastic, who move a lot of books at low prices. Think about your goal. Is it to sell large quantities at a low price, make money at a high price, or just spread the word? Would you rather sell one over-priced book for a $20 royalty or 2000 books for a $1.00 royalty and earn $1000?

Many authors price their books so they can easily discount sale offerings, in-person signings, workshops, or conventions, such as a $12.99 retail price and a $9.99 show special. Some authors prefer to price their books at a low introductory price to get attention and then ramp up the price if their book gets popular. Others price their book so it can be shipped PRIME without the customer having to purchase a minimum amount from Amazon.

Here are two different pricing structures for a 32-page color picture book. One is for a book selling for $12.99, and the other is for a book selling for $10.99.

Authors can check their royalties using the *Royalties Estimator* on the KDP REPORTS page (next to the BOOKSHELF).

KDP royalties, pay schedules, and structures are always subject to change. Here are a few examples using books sold for $12.99 and $10.00 retail.

- KDP sells the book for $12.99 retail
- KDP pays the author a $4.14 royalty

Or, the author can buy the book for $3.65 + shipping and sell it for any price.

- KDP sells the book for $10.00 retail
- KDP pays the author a $2.35 royalty

Or, the author can buy the book for $3.65 + shipping and sell it for any price.

What is your STORY?

Think like your **audience**. No matter who you're writing for, your story should have a beginning, a middle, and a satisfying ending.

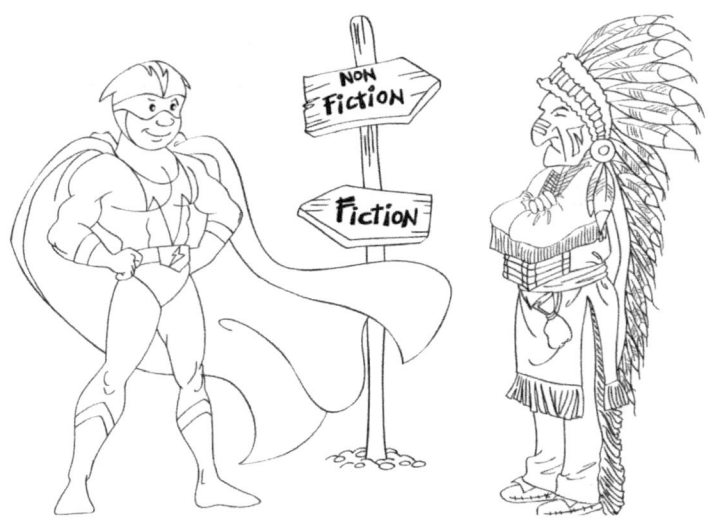

Nonfiction stories are based on facts, real events, and real people, such as a biography or historical story.

FICTION

If your story is **fiction**, then it was created from your imagination. It doesn't matter what the subject of your book is. If you made it up, then it is fiction. A fictional story has the following elements:

- **Plot**: the main events of the story, including the conflict and solution
- **Characters**: the people, animals, or imaginary objects in the story.
- **Setting**: the time and place where the story happens.
- **Theme**: the main message, lesson learned, or moral of the story.

The first thing you need when you write a picture book is a good idea. You will probably come up with many ideas you won't use, but don't give up. Think! An adult caregiver, like a parent or teacher, will be buying the book. Will an adult want to read what you wrote to a child? Is this something they have experienced? Will a child want to listen to what you wrote? What is the moral or life lesson of the story? Are you teaching a child something that's important to know? Are you addressing an issue?

Common THEMES

Pick a theme to which many readers can relate. A **theme** is the main idea or topic of your story. The theme doesn't have to be original. The same issues and life lessons pop up in children's books all of the time. Your success will depend upon how unique and captivating your approach is. You can also come up with a new topic. Tell your story not just to one child but to the masses.

Here are some common themes for children's picture books:

- Words can hurt
- Care for the planet
- Nature and exploration
- Battling fear and anxiety
- Good hygiene
- Moving away
- Mindfulness and self-care
- Feelings and emotions
- Specific illnesses
- Dealing with loss and grief
- A parent's love is endless
- Escape from reality
- Teamwork makes the dream work
- There are different types of families

- Differences can bring us together
- Don't judge a book by its cover
- Community helpers are our friends
- An act of kindness can change a life
- Material possessions are not as important as friendship
- Rumors and gossip can hurt people
- It's what's inside a person that matters
- We are all the same on the inside
- Friendship and belonging
- Work hard for what you want
- Making healthy food choices
- Stay physically active
- Actions have consequences
- Honesty is the best policy
- Practice makes you better
- Trying new things and persistence
- Education is important
- Working hard pays off
- Accepting who you are
- Sharing is caring
- Anti-bullying
- Good sportsmanship
- Problem-solving
- Overcoming adversity
- Never give up
- Patience is a virtue

GENRES

As mentioned before, a **genre** is a particular category of a book, such as mystery, science fiction, fantasy, comedy, love and friendship, thriller, and horror. Choose a genre and be true to it. Fans of certain genres expect to read about specific things. Readers who like horror hope to get scared. Readers who prefer mysteries expect a riddle to decipher or a secret to uncover. Readers who enjoy adventure want an exciting and possibly perilous encounter.

- ACTION
- ADVENTURE
- THRILLER

- SCIENCE FICTION
- TIME TRAVEL
- SPACE EXPLORATION
- ALIENS

- SCIENCE
- DISCOVERY

- MAGIC
- WIZARDRY
- FANTASY
- MYTHICAL CREATURES

- MYSTERY
- CRIME-SOLVING
- PROBLEM-SOLVING

- AREAS of PERSONAL INTEREST
- EXPERIENCES
- REALISTIC FICTION
- HUMOR
- EMOTIONAL ISSUES
- CONCEPT BOOKS
- INTERACTIVE BOOKS
- WORDLESS BOOKS

- NATURE
- ANIMALS
- INSECTS
- BIOGRAPHIES
- Other FACTS

The PLOT

A story doesn't exist without a plot of some kind, and there is no rule that says you have to follow a traditional plot. The **plot** is the storyline of the text or the main events of the story written in sequence. Not all stories are driven forward by a strong plot. As a matter of fact, some authors have broken the rules and found success in doing it. Whatever your plot, it should be easy to follow. Find a way to interest the readers and keep them turning pages, guessing what the next move will be.

Here is an example of a **traditional plot**:

- Introduce the main character.
- Introduce the setting of the story.
- Present the conflict or problem.
- The conflict escalates, or the problem gets worse.
- The character tries to resolve the conflict.
- The conflict is as bad as it can get.
- The character resolves the conflict.

The CHARACTERS

There should be a memorable and well-developed **main character** that is the major focus of the story. It can be a person, an animal, an insect, an alien, or an inanimate object that comes to life. Everything that happens in the story should revolve around and affect the main character in some way. Don't waste words describing a character. That's what there are illustrations on each page.

- The reader wants to care about and cheer for the main character.
- The reader wants to identify with the character's dreams, habits, or choices.
- All characters need to be human-like, believable, convincing, and interesting.
- The behavior of the characters should also be reasonable for their age, knowledge, and background.
- The main character should grow and learn from mistakes, solve the problem, overcome a challenge, make discoveries, and develop over time as people do in real life.

Give people **real-life characteristics** and **actions**. Real people hesitate with uncertainty, rush recklessly into trouble, stutter when they're nervous, shiver when it's cold, wipe their foreheads when it's hot, sneeze from allergies, gesture when they celebrate, jerk when startled - and those are just a few actions. There are thousands.

Describe **feelings** and **emotions** people have in real life. People jump for joy, have nervous tics, zone out under pressure, blush when embarrassed, clench their teeth in anger, have unusual fears, sense something is wrong, shiver with rage, laugh until their cheeks hurt, and cry until they sniffle or hiccup. Characters cry because they're happy, sad, or just emotional. They laugh or giggle when something is funny, but also when they're nervous.

Reporting: *"She was scared."*
Showing: *"Her hands trembled as she peaked through her fingers."*

Reporting: *"He was out of shape."*
Showing: *"He heaved and puffed when he climbed the stairs."*

Reporting: *"He was very tired."*
Showing: *"His crutches rubbed him raw, and his hands grew numb."*

Instead of using words because they sound cool, use them to describe the **correct actions**. Is the bird swooping or hovering? If it is swooping, it's coming down. If it is hovering, it is hanging in the air. Every word a writer uses helps create a picture in the reader's mind. Are readers seeing what you want them to see?

Young children are very impressionable. It's best not to encourage them to do something risky, dangerous, or disrespectful. We don't want children jumping off rooftops, skiing off marked paths, skateboarding without helmets, using swear words, or talking back to their grandmother. Parents don't want to encourage that type of behavior, and they are the ones buying books.

In the book *Come Along, Daisy,* by Jane Simmons, Mama Duck encourages Baby Duck to come along, but Baby Duck wanders off, gets lost, sees frightening things, and eventually finds her way back to her mother. Who can't relate to this story? Certainly, the parents and a lot of little kids.

In the book, *No David*, by David Shannon, a little boy is constantly causing trouble in and around his home. He eventually learns that his mother loves him no matter his behavior.

Supporting characters are characters that are not the main focus of the story but contribute to the story in a significant way. They can have various personality traits. They can be loyal, kind, funny, crazy, helpful, unsympathetic, mean, or generally disliked by the reader, to name a few. Either way, the main character should be reacting to the supporting character's actions and vice versa.

DIVERSITY & INCLUSION

Let's talk for a minute about **diversity** and the **inclusion** of different types of people. Children want to see characters who remind them of themselves. Write about what you know and how you live. Share your culture. Our world is a melting pot of people with different ethnicities, languages, beliefs, cultures, and religions.

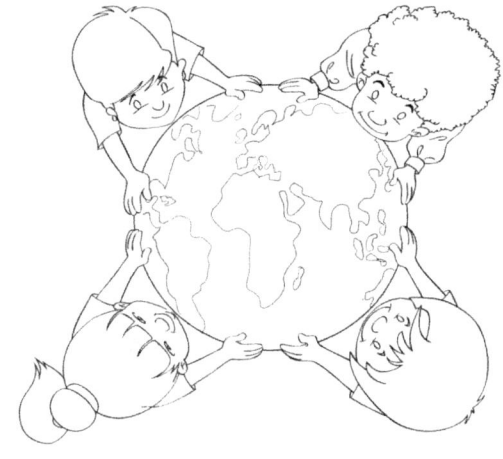

Children need positive affirmations of their identities and self-worth. If the story allows for it, make a conscious effort to include characters and supporting characters that are diverse. Include children who have freckles, an array of skin tones, various hair styles and colors, different body shapes and heights, disabilities or handicaps, wear glasses or braces, speak a foreign language, eat different foods, do things another way, or live differently. You can't please everyone, but diverse and inclusive books help readers learn acceptance and tolerance of others.

Your book may be the only exposure a child gets to other cultures and ways of life.

STEREOTYPES

A **stereotype** is an idea about how people will act based on the group to which they belong. They are often created about people of specific cultures, races, or genders. Look through your book. Do you show only boys skateboarding or playing with cars? Do you show only girls playing with dolls? How would seeing these images influence a child? Almost everyone stereotypes people in some way, without even thinking, but young children are still developing their identities. They shouldn't worry about how the world expects them to think, act, and look. They get enough of that from books, commercials, television shows, games, movies, and, believe it or not, their parents.

There are thousands of stereotypes in hundreds of categories. Here are some examples of **common stereotypes** about genders and families.

- Boys play with trucks, and girls play with dolls.
- Girls wear dresses and boys wear pants.
- Girls watch princess movies, and boys watch superhero movies.
- Boys are wild and active, while girls are quiet and passive.
- Boys take more risks than girls.
- Girls wear their hair long, and boys cut theirs short.
- Only girls wear ponytails.
- Only girls paint their nails.
- Boys never cry. Girls get emotional.
- Boys are messy, and women are clean.
- Boys play with boys, and girls play with girls.
- Girls worry about how they look, and boys don't.
- Boys don't wear pink.
- Girls are not good at sports.
- Only men support the family financially.
- Only men use tools and repair cars.
- Only moms do home chores and take care of the kids.
- The assumption that every parent has a professional vs. a blue-collar job.
- The assumption that every child has two parents or a traditional family structure.

Children learn from the roles they see boys and girls play at home, in books, in film, and in other media to which they are exposed. Look at your illustration with an eye toward portraying girls and boys in ways that encourage them to be who they want to be. Can you change the gender of a character from a boy to a girl or vice versa without it affecting your story? If you can, then do so. We illustrated a girl riding a skateboard on the previous page instead of a boy because it is considered atypical.

Be careful of cultural stereotypes, as well. People from one culture often categorize people from another culture. Beliefs like African Americans are poor, only Asians stir fry, or all Native Americans wear animal skins are formed out of ignorance.

SETTING

You can't write a story that happens nowhere. The **setting** is the place or type of surroundings where the story takes place, so the illustration should provide visual cues for the reader. The illustration is supposed to show the reader the setting; you shouldn't have to describe it in the text like you would in a novel. Let the text focus on the action of the story, flow through the events, and drive the dialogue.

Since young children experience their world differently from adults, they require settings to which they can relate personal experiences, such as at home, the park, a carnival, school, sports fields, dance class, a farm, a movie theater, etc. With that in mind, you also want to give children new experiences. Start with the familiar and expand their relationship to the rest of the world, whether it be real or fantasy. Taking children out of the space they know will make the book much more entertaining.

- *Where the Wild Things Are,* by Maurice Sendak, takes a child out of the house for a wild, fantastical visit to the jungle where the wild creatures are, then brings the child back to the comfort and security of home.

- *Hair Love,* by Matthew A. Cherry, is a book about an African American father challenged to style his daughter's wild hair.

- *If You Give a Mouse a Cookie*, by Laura Numeroff, introduces an adorable stubborn little mouse who takes a child through a sequence of events in the home.

- *Fruits and Veggies Row by Row*, by Angela Russ-Ayon, introduces children to planting fruits and vegetables in a garden from the children's perspective.

- *The Colors of Us*, by Karen Katz, tours children around the neighborhood looking for people with different skin tones.

DIALOG

A story benefits from having **dialog**, or a conversation between two or more characters. Stories without dialog can be very dull. Readers love listening in on other people's conversations. That's why gossip is so popular. Put words into the mouths of your characters that sound real and are the way children actually talk and think. The words characters speak should be age-appropriate, make sense, and be consistent with how characters would respond and what they would typically say based on their ages, experiences, and backgrounds. For example, a typical four-year-old would not be able to describe his rocket in scientific terms.

Dialog can move the storyline along by revealing relevant and meaningful information the reader didn't know, such as the mood, relationships, the setting, backstory, etc.

Read your story to friends and other children to get their reaction to what your characters are saying.

Authors use all **five senses** to bring the reader into the story. Whatever your character is seeing, hearing, touching, smelling, and tasting, the reader is also. Sight is the most important sense in descriptive writing, but don't leave the others out - ordinary, everyday sounds transport readers into a scene. Smells can trigger emotions and memories just as well.

Here are some examples of writing using the five senses :

- *The waft of his cologne stung her eyes.*
- *Her laugh pierced his ears with its high pitch.*
- *His tattoo coiled in the shape of a striking snake.*
- *The odor of rotting fish on the boat made her gag.*
- *The wind carried the scent of coconut oil and seaweed.*
- *She licked her lips and tasted the tang of salt in the air.*
- *Rain tapped against the window, like fingers drumming on glass.*
- *The zipline snapped like a bolt of lightning.*
- *When she clenched her fists, he took a step back.*
- *He knew he was late when the crickets began to chirp.*
- *His firm handshake nearly broke her bones.*
- *By the fifth bite of the spicy dish, she'd lost all feeling in her taste buds.*

NONFICTION

Your book is **nonfiction** if it is **based on facts**, which is the broadest category of literature. The goal of nonfiction is to provide information based on the author's expertise or research, as opposed to fiction, which is based on the author's imagination and creativity. Classroom textbooks, autobiographies, memoirs or life stories, encyclopedias, essays based on research, dictionaries, thesauruses, news or interview articles, and educational didactic books are all nonfiction. An autobiography may have a plot, depending on how detailed the account is. Non-fiction books are meant to inform, persuade, and, if well-written, entertain.

DIDACTIC BOOKS

Educational didactic picture books are designed to teach the reader something. This type of book may not have any characters, dialogue, or story elements.

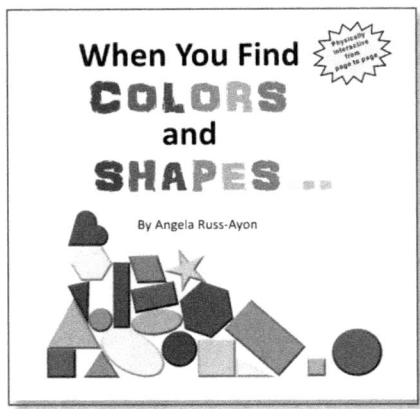

When You Find Colors and Shapes, by Angela Russ-Ayon, is a picture book that encourages children to move as directed every time they locate a shape of a specific color. The goal of the book is to teach young children about shapes and colors, while also getting them up and moving. There is no main character, and there is no plot in the book.

Have you written a didactic book with educational or message-driven concepts? If you remove the lesson or moral at the end of your story, and the story falls into an abyss, then your book is didactic. There is no character who faces a conflict, overcomes it, and learns something.

There is nothing wrong with didactic books, especially those that capture and keep a child's attention. Didactic books should instruct AND entertain if at all possible. Many parents and educators use didactic books to teach concepts, but think about how you might introduce the subject matter using an interesting story with a traditional plot structure. You don't want to manipulate a child's emotions by telling them how to feel, think, and learn. You want to allow children to bring their own feelings and ideas to the text through independent thinking, discoveries, open-ended discussions, and engaging extensions.

You might see books like these on subjects such as the alphabet, emotions, colors, number sense and math concepts, science, the food pyramid, gardening, cooking, building something, and so forth. Nonfiction books can often be pitched to publishers in the form of proposals, rather than finished manuscripts.

The WORDS in a STORY

Self-published authors usually write manuscripts first and then illustrate them after their stories are complete. A **manuscript** is an original book that has not been published. The **text** is the original words in the story.

People think writing picture books is easy, but it can be challenging. Writing is a skill that gets better with practice. Even the most seasoned writers take classes and workshops to improve their craft, and they write all of the time.

Bait the hook on the first page and imaginatively lead readers through the story. What's the catch? Here are a few examples from popular picture books:

- *The Day the Crayons Quit,* by Drew Dewalt - Children want to keep turning pages to see what the crayons will complain about next.

- *Never, EVER Shout in a Zoo*, by Karma Wilson - The first line warns children not to shout because anything might happen. Of course, they want to shout and see what happens.

- *It's a Book*, by Lane Smith - The first line, "What do you have there?" attracts the reader who wants to hear answers to the character's questions.

These are perfect examples of why studying popular children's books can be so helpful when it comes to writing your own.

It's never too late to improve your book when you self-publish by print-on-demand with KDP, but you should revisit, review, edit, and revise your work until you know it is the best it can be before you publish and give the public access to it.

Ask yourself if you actually need all of the words you used. Are they interesting? Are they fun to say? Do they add to your story? Can you change them in order to incorporate the senses? It's okay to teach young children new words and give them a rich language experience. That's how they learn new vocabulary, but they should easily understand most of the words in the book. If there is a list somewhere of words you should use in children's books, it is probably way too long to be helpful to writers.

Show readers how the character feels, by their actions, reactions, gestures, facial expressions, and dialogue. No one gets emotional when they read a report about how a character feels. Take a day to observe children. Examine how they react and respond to things. Put yourself in the shoes of the characters and act out the scenes.

Move the story along, rather than dwelling so long on one event that the reader loses interest. Also, avoid unnecessary and unrelated details that stop the momentum of your story. Ask yourself, "What is important in this scene?" A child who is lying in bed, afraid of the dark, is not going to be thinking about what he'll eat for lunch tomorrow.

Keep children within your fictional world with realistic and logical scenes, problems, and solutions. A character who needs to escape a situation doesn't simply step into a rocket and fly to the moon.

Don't just write to be writing. Every word in a sentence serves a specific purpose, and every sentence gives a story meaning. Complicated sentence structure is not age-appropriate for pre-readers. Look at how popular the book *Hop on Pop,* by Dr. Seuss, is filled with simple two and three-letter words for early readers.

Be conscious of your audience. Books for babies and toddlers have words that are mostly limited to one or two syllables. Books for young children might also introduce longer, more complex words that help them identify objects, animals, and insects. Children are introduced to longer, multi-syllable words as they grow older. Sit and listen to how they respond to their environment and experiences. What do they say? How do they speak? They don't talk like adults.

Look over your work for repeated words. Find different ways to say things. You have 30 pages or fewer, and with over 170,000 words in a typical English Dictionary, you shouldn't have to repeat yourself. Some grammar programs will red-flag overused words, and a thesaurus will help you find synonyms.

Creatively engage your audience!

◊ In the picture book *Dinousaurumpus*, by Tony Mitton, the author repeats a phrase every few pages that encourages readers to get up and stomp around like dinosaurs. Children anxiously await the phrase that gives them permission to stand and act silly.

◊ In the African folktale, *Abiyoyo*, by Pete Seeger, children are encouraged to sing a chant that will put the fearsome giant to sleep.

◊ In *The Colors of Us*, by Karen Katz, children try to match their skin tone to those in the illustration.

◊ In *Brown Bear, Brown Bear, What Do You See?,* by Bill Martin, keeps children guessing which animal will come next.

Finally, your work should be yours and yours alone. Taking someone else's work is called **plagiarism**, and is just like stealing someone's possessions. You can't claim someone else's idea or train of thought as your own, copy someone's work without giving them credit, or use a direct quote or paraphrase without citing the source.

WORD COUNT

The **word count** is the total number of words in a book, from the beginning of the story to the end. A picture book for preschoolers might have 50 to 600 words from cover to back, whereas a book for second graders would have a more complex vocabulary with a word count ranging from 1000 to 1500. These ranges vary, depending on who you ask.

Writing programs like WORD, Google Docs, or PAGES have an option where you can highlight the words and check the word count.

POINT of VIEW

Keep to one point of view. A **point of view (POV)** is the opinions or feelings of a person involved in your story. The POV is what determines how readers "hear" and "see" what takes place in a story. Once you decide who will tell your story to the reader, stick with that person or point of view. There are three major kinds of POV.

1. **First-Person:** With this POV, someone is telling the reader his or her story, including thoughts, opinions, emotions, actions, and so on. Telling a story using this POV involves using the pronouns "I" and "we." Here are a few examples.

*"**I** liked to stand in the corner and watch people."*

*"**I** will never not ever eat a tomato."*

*"**I** am just a little boy. How would **I** know how to do that?"*

*"**We** turned over the timer every time **we** took a turn."*

2. **Second-Person:** With this POV, the reader is invited to participate in the story and learns page by page what happens as a result of his or her actions. The author or narrator of the story speaks directly to the reader, telling the reader how to do something. Second-person P.O.V. is popular with books that teach, guide, warn, or instruct the reader. This POV involves using the pronoun "you."

Here are a few examples.

*"If **you** give a mouse a cookie,..."*

*"**You** don't know what **you**'ve got until it's gone."*

*"To make lemonade, **you** combine lemon juice, water, and sugar."*

*"Maybe **you** should put this book back. **You** don't want to let the monkeys out."*

3. Third-Person: With a third person POV, the readers feel like someone is holding a camera and filming the events, or like they are listening to people gossip. Telling the story using this POV involves using pronouns like "he," "she," "it," "they," or a person's name. Here are a few examples.

*"**She** went out through the back door, and that's when **she** saw it."*

*"**He** was an honest young man. That's why **he** gave the money back."*

*"**She** would not tell her little brother how the bad man took the snowman's nose."*

*"**They** shared a secret about their new dog and didn't want to tell anyone."*

GRAMMAR

Grammar is the set of rules that explains how words change their form and combine with other words in a language. It doesn't matter whether you're writing fiction or nonfiction. No matter how creative you are, there are rules of grammar you must follow when you write, like capitalizing the first word in every sentence, proper punctuation, and using words correctly.

Free web-based programs like **Scribens.com** and fee-based computer applications like **Grammarly.com** review your work for common mistakes such as punctuation, sentence structure, missing words, common typos, article use (a, an, the), and subject-verb agreement.

You can also hire a professional **copyeditor** or line editor to check your sentence structure, story structure, details, and facts. Whereas a **proofreader** corrects typographical errors, grammar mistakes, and may also look for inaccurate facts.

< See more tips on the "PROOFREADING" page. >

RHYMING

Rhyming is when a word, syllable, or end of a line has the same sound as another. Children's books don't have to rhyme, but if you want your book to rhyme, you should write perfect rhymes, not words that almost rhyme, called **near rhymes,** half rhymes, or imperfect rhymes. Near rhymes are very popular in mainstream songs, but are not appropriate for young children who are still learning to read. For example, a perfect rhyme is meat/feet/neat. Both the "ee" sound and the ending "t" sound match perfectly. Similarly, note/boat/tote share both the "oh" sound and the ending "t" sound at the end. However, near rhymes such as note/spoke, or life/dice, share the same middle sounds, but not the same endings. Imperfect rhymes such as sting/sharing have "ing" endings, but are off-rhythm and focus on different stress points.

Exact rhymes:
land, sand, band
dice, mice, nice
same, name, came
cat, bat, hat

As opposed to:
land, man, ham
dice, kite, pipe
same, Jane, pain
cat, lap, bag

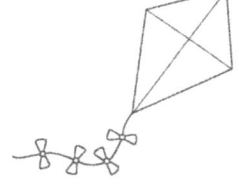

Write your story first, then work on the rhyming. One of the best rhymers in the history of children's books was Dr. Seuss, even though he rhymed many words that made no sense. If you read a book out loud, you'll probably be able to notice a rhythm, or a beat, running through it, as you would hear in a song. If the rhyme is off, the phrases will sound awkward, like a hiccup. Rhyming should

blend into the story and flow naturally, with a repetitive, measured syllable count to which you can play a drum. It helps to clap out the syllables of each line to make sure they are steady and consistent.

Whether you rhyme every line, every other line, or even every fourth line, be consistent. Rhyming takes practice. Consider a repeating rhyming phrase. If you decide to use near rhymes, do it throughout your whole book. Don't bounce back and forth. Your book may not rhyme perfectly, but it will sound nice. The story is more important than the rhyme. If your attempts to rhyme are messing up the story, then abandon the rhyming altogether.

Here are some helpful tips for becoming a better writer:

- Read, read, and read some more, especially the genre you want to write.
- Write all of the time. Practice makes writing better.
- Build your own personal reference book or PDF library.
- Research the most common misspelled words.
- Get your facts straight. Do your research, especially if you are writing a nonfiction book.
- Attend writing workshops and online webinars.

If you aren't sure about grammar or how to use a particular word, turn to a source such as a dictionary or a thesaurus. Most computer writing programs have spell-checks, and you can visit a local library, or use online search engines like Google for assistance.

LET's RECAP about WRITING the MANUSCRIPT

- Be conscious of your audience.
- Use simple sentence structure for early readers.
- Show with actions, reactions, facial expressions, gestures, and dialogue. Don't just report and tell.
- Describe feelings and emotions in creative ways.
- Use descriptive words correctly, not just because you like them.
- Use all five senses.
- Consistent perfect rhymes, near rhymes, or none at all.
- Watch your word count. Do you really need all of those words?
- Look out for repeated words.
- Give characters real-life traits to which children can relate.
- Keep to one point of view.
- Make sure the events in your story are in the right order.
- Move the story along so readers don't get bored.
- No plagiarizing.
- Avoid risky, dangerous, or disrespectful storylines.
- Check for grammatical errors and misspelled words. Use grammar programs and applications.
- Hire a copyeditor or proofreader to check your story.
- Join a writer's critique group for feedback.

Fiction STORY MAP

A **story map** helps writers organize their thoughts by filling in the elements of a book or story and identifying the story's characters, plot, setting, problem, and solution. There are many different types of story maps. Here are three simplified versions for fiction:

Title:

_____

Author:

_____

Main Characters:

_____

Setting:

_____

Statement of the Problem:

_____

Summary of the Beginning of the Story or First Attempt to Problem Solve:

_____

Summary of the Middle of the Story or Second Attempt to Problem Solve:

_____

Summary of the Ending of the Story or Third Attempt to Problem Solve:

_____

How the Problem is Solved • Dramatic moment that directly relates to the problem:

_____

Story Theme • Main Idea (What general message is the author telling the reader?):

_____

Fiction STORY MAP

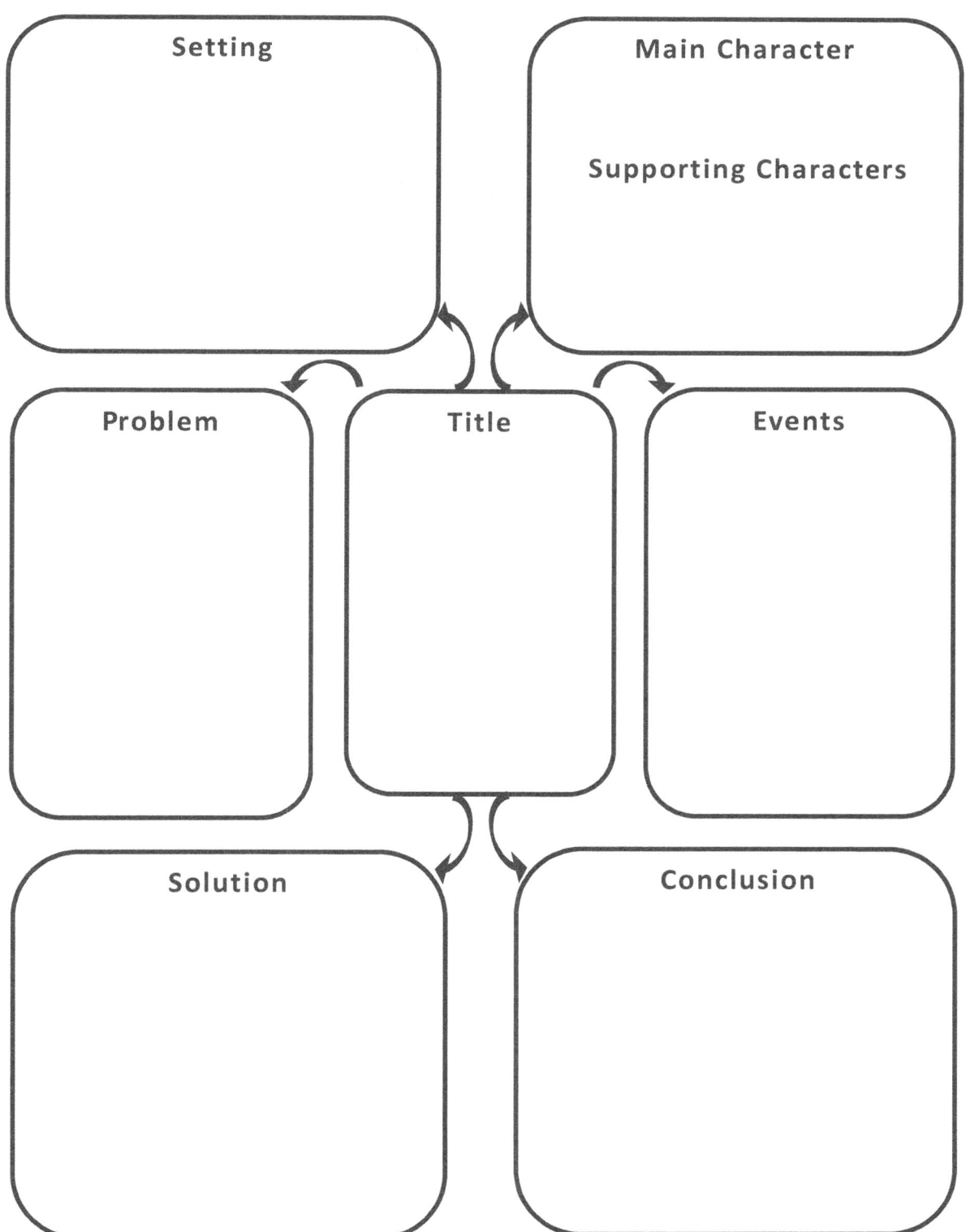

Setting

Main Character

Supporting Characters

Problem

Title

Events

Solution

Conclusion

How to Self-Publish a Children's Picture Book

Fiction STORY MAP

Setting

Characters

Beginning

Problem or Conflict

Solution

Nonfiction STORY MAP

Subject or Topic

Purpose
Persuade • Inform

Research • Background Information • Details

Examples

Drawings • Diagrams

Conclusion

Nonfiction STORY MAP

Who?

What?

When?

Where?

Why?

How?

EDITING

When you **edit** a book, you check, correct, modify, and rearrange the work. Copyediting is the stage of writing when you improve clarity, accuracy, consistency, and grammar. It requires reading, re-writing, re-reading, re-writing, and re-reading your work over and over again. Even the best writers revise their stories multiple times. Editing involves making all kinds of corrections.

Here are some main issues for which to look:

- Filling in gaps and holes in the story.
- Making sure the story and scenes flow smoothly from one idea to the next.
- Rearranging sentences, paragraphs, illustrations, pages, etc.
- Correcting tenses.
- Writing in a consistent point of view.
- Removing unnecessary or inappropriate words.
- Checking for errors in punctuation, grammar, and spelling, including omitted or incorrect use of words.
- Ensuring text formats, line spacing, indents, formatted pictures, and margins are consistent.
- Fact-checking things like dates, times, names, historical facts, locations, computations, and other details.
- Filling in headlines, headers, photo captions, charts, or summaries.
- Double-checking illustrations, diagrams, or photos for usage rights and correct resolution.
- Any numbering (bullets) is numerical.
- The pages are in the correct numerical order.

Take a step back from your story for a week or so. When you reread it, read it out loud, checking for one issue at a time.

- Ask family, friends, and associates who you respect to review your work.
- Listen to positive, helpful, constructive criticism, without insult.
- Ignore the opinions of people who are negative or who discourage you from writing.
- Take command of your story, and be prepared to make changes. If your story doesn't flow well or make sense, revise it. Be willing to cut text and let go.

< See more tips on the "PROOFREADING" page. >

ILLUSTRATION

An **illustration** is **artwork** or a picture used to clarify and complement your story. Picture books earned their name because of the fun, lush, unique, and captivating illustration that help tell each story. It's the illustration that grabs the interest of children and keeps them wanting to turn to the next page.

If you are going to self-publish a picture book, you have four options:

- illustrate your book
- get someone to illustrate for free
- buy licenses to use photos or illustrations
- pay someone to illustrate your story

If you choose to illustrate, develop your own unique style. There are books illustrated using collages, torn-up cardboard, crayon, and basic black lines. It wouldn't hurt to take a few art classes or read books on how to draw.

You cannot just use any artwork or clip art you find on the internet. Nor can you take an image you find in a Google search or scan an image you like from another book or magazine. That is called **copyright infringement**. Someone else owns that work, and you can't use another person's artwork without asking permission or paying for the right to use it (licensing) if you plan to sell your book.

You can't use images you "find" unless they are **commercial-free, copyright-free,** or in the **public domain.** These categories mean the image <u>can be</u> used to market, promote, or sell your book to make money. They are free for public use and are not subject to copyright, which means you can do what you want with them. Be sure to read the fine print and keep a record of where you found the images in case you are challenged. The main issue with using random images is that the artwork in the book won't look consistent - as if one person did all of the pictures.

A lot of what you find on the internet is not the proper resolution for quality printing. Even if you obtain the right to use artwork, **any image you use for printing or publishing has to be at a hi-resolution** meant for "High Quality" or "Commercial Press," which is 300 dpi or higher. When you get your proof, check for fuzzy images.

If you choose an artist to illustrate your book, pick someone who has a style you like and uses a **medium** (or way of completing the artwork) you prefer, such as watercolors, colored pencils, acrylic paint, crayons, ink, or pencil, or pastels. Most artists specialize in only one or two mediums, and that's how they do their best work. **You want your artwork to be consistent throughout your book.** For example, your book won't look uniform if some pages are illustrated with watercolor and others are crayon drawings, or if some illustrations are outlined with thick lines and other outlines are thin. Your color images should have the same style and appearance as if they were all done by the same illustrator.

There are different ways to complete the illustration. Artists produce artwork on tablets using drawing programs, directly on a computer using illustration software, or on paper or canvas that will have to be scanned. **Amazon KDP prints from digital files**, so the artwork has to be digital, too. In other words, no matter how the illustration is completed, it has to be eventually uploaded to KDP from a computer.

Inspiration is everywhere. Look through other picture books, magazines, websites, social media, television, movies, and trending articles.

Writers visualize how they want their illustration to look, like a movie playing in their heads. Draw and sketch until you end up with what you think you want, even if it's only to give an artist an idea of what you want. Just keep in mind that if someone else illustrates your story, the artwork may not come out like you pictured it in your head.

Begin the artwork by sketching out your ideas using simple drawings. Even stick figure drawings are okay. Sketch out each page and arrange the pages in a **logical order**, building a storyboard.

A **storyboard** is an easy way to organize your story using small rough illustrations in sequence. Read your storyboard out loud to see how the text and illustration flow. You might find you need to rearrange, delete, or modify the story, illustrations, or sequence of pages. Storyboards are provided at the end of this book.

Leave plenty of room for the text, or it will have to be placed over important features in the illustration. If you plan to translate your book into other languages, you may need additional room on each page. Many educators like to read the foreign language and the English translation on the same page.

The fun is in the details! Mix things up! Since books are read again and again, it's nice to provide the reader with levels of illustrated detail. Plan your artwork in such a way that if the book is read more than once, and it usually is, readers have something new to discover, such as hidden insects or animals, identifiable images in the pictures hanging on the walls, an array of recognizable toys in the playroom, surprise hidden faces, food in the open refrigerator, labels and signs in the background, etc.

Offer more to discover and discuss. Young children are still learning about everything: numbers, the alphabet, colors, shapes, sizes, living and nonliving things, simple machines, etc. Look at a page from the ocean story below. This picture gives children a lot to talk about. They can identify fish, count fish/ bubbles/seaweed, compare characteristics of ocean creatures (dolphin, whale, other fish, crab, seahorse), contrast between fish and humans, discuss positions in space (top, bottom, beside, behind, over, under, etc.), and so forth. The placement of the text is just an example.

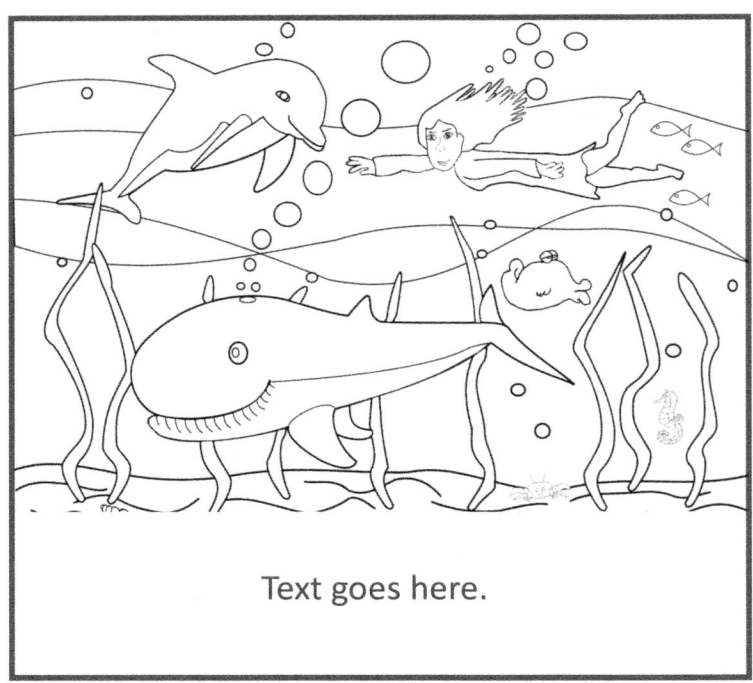

Text goes here.

A book also flows much better if the illustrated pages have changes in **perspective**. Perspective is the way readers see and experience the events and feelings in a story. In art, it's a way of drawing objects to give the reader a particular view. You can do this in a few different ways, but the most common for picture books is to:

- go from busy with a lot of activity to idle with nothing much happening.

- go from loud images with a lot of detail to quiet images with not much detail at all.

- change the viewpoint. Give readers scenes from different angles. Take them far away, bring them up close, or fly them overhead. Shoot the scene from behind or in profile.

Here is an example of two different viewpoints. One displays blueberries close up, and the other has an entire blueberry bush and character from far away. They are placed opposite of each other in the story.

You don't need to constantly switch back and forth from one perspective to another, but adding different perspectives here and there makes the book visually appealing. A common mistake is to try to do too much when less does the job. Any illustration that is overly busy distracts readers because they will have no idea where to look, or bores readers with repetitive imagery.

The illustration should flow from left to right, the same way people read. Think of it as cars all moving in the same direction. Rotate characters that are facing left to the right for a more comfortable read.

Give illustration a human element using a person's entire body or body parts. You want children to walk for a few minutes in the same shoes as the characters in your story. Have you ever watched children play? One child isn't interested in a toy until another child picks it up. You want the reader interested in picking up that toy, too. Do you see the difference between the two images below from *We Eat Food That's Fresh,* by Angela Russ-Ayon? Which image inspires children to prepare and serve food in a fun and unique way, and maybe even try something new?

Show, don't tell. The pictures are supposed to tell the story and support the text, not mirror what was just read. If you are saying in words what is obvious to a reader who is looking at the illustration, focus on some other aspect of what is taking place. What is evident in the illustration does not have to be said in words. For instance, instead of telling the reader that the children discovered a box when that is obvious in the picture, focus on how the children feel about the discovery.

Avoid illustration that shows the opposite of what you have written unless you are creatively writing an entire book about opposites. If you write about how a girl is jumping for joy, then the illustration shouldn't show her sitting down.

Ask a friend or mentor to look at your work and see if there is anything you missed. Sometimes there are obvious problems with the illustration or story that aren't

caught until someone points them out. Don't be afraid to share your work. Be receptive and open to ideas that will improve your book. Constructive feedback can improve a book tenfold.

Introduce new concepts on odd-numbered pages. Odd page numbers appear on the right side of the book. Children's picture books don't have page numbers or chapters, but if they did have chapters, they would start on the odd pages.

Review your book in a two-page spread. Make sure your colors, borders, margins, messages, and illustrations are uniform when the book is open in a spread. For instance, if two pages are related, they should be opposite of each other. If the reader is supposed to guess what's on the next page, the answer should require a page turn. Do the borders line up? Does the text start at the same level? Do the colors match on each side?

Insert images into files at their original size; don't cut and paste. After you insert your images, only enlarge them if they are high-resolution images because doing so will decrease their resolution.

To reduce a file's size, some programs, such as Microsoft Word or Publisher, are set to compress images. **Turn off image compression** in your computer program.

FORMATTING ARTWORK

The **artwork** is the pictures and illustrations in the book. Whether the artwork is completed digitally or scanned from an original, images and illustrations have to be a **hi-resolution** of 300 dpi (dots per inch) or higher. If you publish your book with low-resolution artwork, the images will come out blurry and pixelated, even if it looks good on your computer. Some self-publishing companies will warn you that your artwork isn't the right resolution in the review process. KDP doesn't always catch this problem.

300 dpi hi-resolution cupcake (sharp)

low-resolution cupcake (fuzzy)

Original artwork for KDP should be in CMYK colors, which is standard in the printing industry. CMYK is a color model for combining primary pigments. The C stands for cyan (aqua), M stands for magenta (pink), Y for yellow, and K for Key. Set your design program to work in CMYK before you begin adding color to your illustration. Computers use RGB (Red, Green, Blue) color values, so what you see on your computer monitor may not be what you see in CMYK after the book is printed.

C = Cyan
M = Magenta
Y = Yellow
K = Black

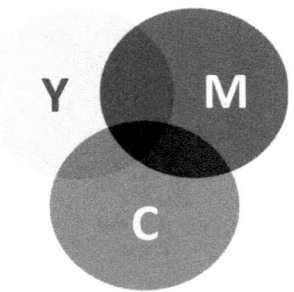

Although KDP will also print RGB colors, RGB is not recommended for producing true colors in KDP books. RGB stands for "Red, Green, Blue." It refers to the three hues of light, that can mix together to form any color. **When using CMYK there are fewer color possibilities** than with RGB, so, unfortunately, you can't reproduce many of the vibrant RGB colors with CMYK. When illustrations are colorized using RGB colors, the printer who uses CMYK is forced to do a "best guess" to match colors.

R = Red   G = Green   B = Blue

COLORS

The Premium color option on KDP is ideal for image-heavy color interiors, like children's books, where image sharpness and clarity is essential.

◊ The perfect printed proof you receive may not look the same as the copies ordered directly on Amazon.com because proofs are not printed on the same equipment as the final KDP print-on-demand copies you sell.

◊ Do not rely solely on your monitor to test the CMYK colors. Monitor images are backlit and will appear brighter than printed images. Print the book's cover on a desktop color printer using photo paper and compare it to the printed proof in different lighting, including the sun.

Pay close attention to your color palette, or range of colors. A color palette might include earth tones such as brown, burgundy, cream, and dark green. Maybe you like bright, bold colors like crimson red, orange, and sunshine yellow. Whatever colors you choose, you want them to flow harmoniously through the pages. If the pages of your book all came apart, would someone be able to easily identify which pages belong to your book because of your use of color, tone, and artistic style? Also, each character and object in your book should have a consistent color palette.

KDP allows for a small percentage of color variation in printing. Color variance is the potential for colors to vary in shades. Variances are often caused by environmental and mechanical factors that are not related to the art files, but it's hard to know whether the color is off because the KDP printer didn't calibrate the equipment properly, or because the book itself has issues. Order a proof to see how your book will print.

Color profiles are color management added to an image or file to help standardize what your colors look like across different screens. **They can produce unexpected results and are automatically removed before publishing by KDP.**

Spot colors, which are generated from ink chosen from a color system, such as the Pantone Matching system, are used in offset printing and **are not compatible with KDP's print-on-demand model.**

Color spaces describe color numerically. **KDP doesn't recommend using multiple color spaces in a file** because it can cause color variance and unexpected printing results.

LAYERING & FLATTENING

When illustrating in most design programs, artists place one layer over another. They might draw a shirt, which would be the first layer, then draw a cat and lay it on the shirt. The cat would be the 2nd layer. The two combined make a composition: a shirt with a cat on it. Before uploading any artwork, images should be flattened or combined into one layer. In doing so, you will no longer be able to manipulate individual layers or edit different elements of an image with filters or editing tools, so always save a copy of your original work.

When you scan original artwork, you won't layer until you place in a **text box**. A text box adds another layer that might need to be flattened or combined. Layers can cause the file to print with missing, distorted, or discolored content. Flattening will also reduce the file size to make it easy to transfer for printing. If you don't know what you're doing, saving your pages as commercial press PDFs will usually flatten the work.

Layer 1	Layer 2	=	Composition

 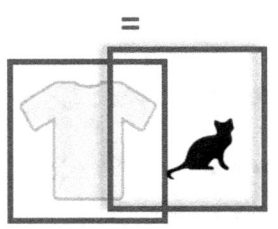 

This formatting section is just a quick overview. There is a lot to know when it comes to the artwork. Ask for help, search the internet, take an online tutorial, or take a class to learn more. In the end, it is up to you to request a printed proof of your book to make sure the images are flattened, in focus, and color correct.

MARGINS

Margins are the areas immediately adjacent to the edges of each page that protect text and illustration from running off the page and being cut off during the printing process. Set up files with consistent margins equidistant from the edge of the pages throughout the book. One-inch margins all around is a good guide.

The **gutter** is the inside margin of a bound book or the middle of a two-page spread. Keep important features and illustrations away from the **inside margins or gutter**. If you run a face across the middle of a spread, you will lose some of the facial detail in the gutter, like a nose, when the book is bound. Make sure the illustration on the left and right sides of the gutter lines up in your software and that the gutter is dead center on the spread.

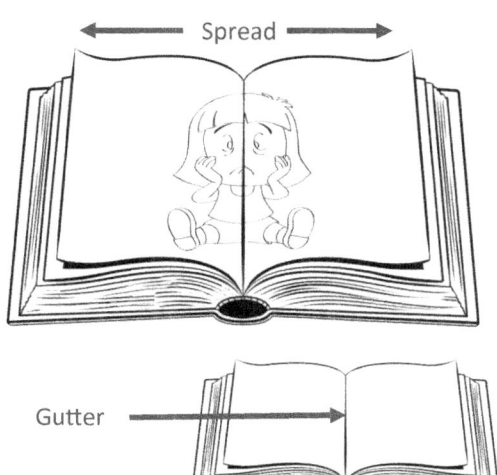

Spread

Gutter

The top, bottom, and outside trim margins must be a minimum of 0.25 inches for books without a **bleed** and 0.375 inches (9.6mm) for books with a bleed (color or text that runs to the edge). The bleed is printing that goes beyond the edge of where the pages are trimmed, as opposed to pages with white borders.

< See more tips on the "BLEED" page. >

The higher the page count, the thicker the book. The thicker the book, the thicker the spine, and the greater the inside margin.

Place essential images and features away from the **outside margins** where they can be cut off. Keep images and text out of the safe area, which is at least another one -half inch in from the margin of the page all around, for good measure. You don't want to lose parts of faces or other interesting things children will want to see when the pages are cut. You also don't want the text to be so close to the gutter that the reader has to press the book open to see the text.

The PARTS of a BOOK

The **cover** of a book is the thick protective outer part on the front that displays the title, an image that will attract a buyer, and the name of the author and illustrator. Paperback books, also known as "soft covers," have a wraparound cover that is rigid, laminated cardstock. Cardstock is stiffer than the paper used for the interior pages, and it's flexible.

Here are some samples of book covers. Design your own cover or create a cover using KDP's Cover Creator tool, which supplies free stock images you can use.

There is a phrase, "Don't judge a book by its cover," which means don't judge something or someone by their outward appearance. But we do judge books by their covers. Yours should send a clear message to buyers, with a big bold title that readers can see clearly when the **thumbnail** (smaller) images appear on Amazon. Design a cover that makes readers curious enough to pick up the book. Your book's genre and mood should be obvious. Your goal should be to grab attention and stop buyers in their tracks.

The **back** of a book is the thick protective outer part you see when you flip over the book. It includes a written description summarizing the book. People usually pick up a book because of the cover and then turn it over to see what it's about on the back. A well-written description draws the buyer in, and if the buyer is still interested, he or she might start flipping through pages to investigate further.

Along with the description, a **barcode** is placed on the back of the book. It identifies the International Standard Book Number (ISBN), and sometimes the price, but we will go over that later.

Here are a few examples of the backs of books. You don't have to put artwork on the back of a book, but it does make the book more appealing.

The PARTS of a BOOK

Interior Pages

Back   Cover

Spine

The cover and back of a book are connected at the spine. The **spine** of a book is the outside edge where the pages are gathered and bound. The spine secures the pages and acts as a hinge that allows the book to open and close without losing the pages. Typically, the spine is the first part of a book people see when it's sitting on a shelf, but some books are not thick enough to print text on the spine. The words would be too small to read. In addition, the printing could shift when the book is trimmed and bound. **KDP will not print text on the spine of books under 79 pages**, so don't worry about fitting text along the spine of your children's picture book.

A **spread** is a pair of facing pages, typically the left- and right-hand pages. An easy way to understand this is by opening a book and pressing it flat against a table so the book is spread out.

SPREAD

BACK and COVER

Back   **Cover**

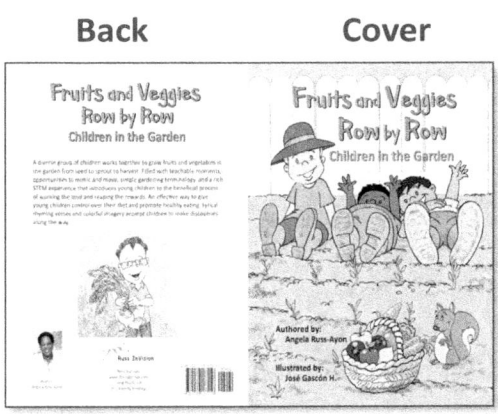

At KDP, the cover and back of the book can be printed in full color or black and white. It is up to you. There is no additional cost for Amazon KDP to print the cover and back in color, even if the interior pages are black and white.

The cover can be printed with either a **glossy** and shiny, or **matte** and flat **finish**. Both are nice, but a shiny finish doesn't show as many fingerprints and scratches as a matte finish. On glossy covers, the color black appears darker and the artwork is more striking. Glossy is pretty standard for textbook, picture book, and novel covers.

INTERIOR PAGES

When Amazon KDP's team refers to **interior pages**, they are talking about the pages you turn on the inside of the book. The interior pages of your book can be black and white or color. Children's picture books are usually printed in color. You can't save money by reducing the number of color interior pages in the book. You can print 29 pages in black and white and one page in color, but including that one color page means the entire interior of the book has to be printed in color. Obviously, it costs more to print picture books in color than in black and white.

Paper Color: KDP interior pages can be printed in black and white, standard color, or premium color. For a children's full-color picture book, select **Premium Color Interior with White Paper.** Amazon KDP allows you to print on white or cream paper if you have black and white interior pages, but it limits you to white paper for color interiors to give you the best contrast between the printed text, the artwork, and the background of the page. For color books, white paper makes the pages easier to read. Besides, if you print color on cream paper, the colors won't come out as crisp and clear. **NOTE:** Premium Color paper limits the size book you can use for expanded distribution.

The **weight** of the **paper** refers to the thickness of a book's paper stock. Amazon KDP does not give you a choice of paper weight. If you feel the cover of a paperback book and then touch the interior pages of the same book, you will feel a difference in the thickness or weight of the paper. Print-on-demand (POD) paperweight can range from about 50 to 70 pounds. They offer standard paper weights for black and white or color books that are always subject to change.

If you sell a large number of books, it might be cost-effective to print them using a professional offset printer in the U.S. or an overseas printer rather than using KDP. You will get a choice of paper weight, but the difference in paper weight will affect the cost of printing with an offset printer. Always request paper samples of the cover and interior pages.

< See more information on the "KDP PRINT RUNS" page. >

Now that your manuscript is complete,

Let's RECAP about the ILLUSTRATION

1. Decide who will illustrate your picture book.
2. Do not use someone else's artwork without permission.
3. Build a roughly sketched storyboard, laying out your illustration ideas in sequence. Be open to the illustrator's ideas.
4. Revise, rewrite, and rearrange your work.
5. Revisit your text to see if it is supported by the illustrations.
6. Select an artistic style and stick with it.
7. Choose a medium and stick with it.
8. Be consistent with your color palette.
9. Colors for KDP should be in CMYK.
10. Check the resolution of your images, pictures, or illustration. (300 dpi)
11. Flatten layers.
12. The fun is in the details!
13. Use all five senses in the illustration, too.
14. Include diverse characters.
15. Watch out for stereotypes.
16. Offer more for the children to discover and discuss.
17. Illustrations should not duplicate what is written. Remove text that is redundant and shown in the illustration.
18. The illustration should not represent the opposite of what is written.
19. Tell your story from different illustrated perspectives.
20. Keep characters and action flowing to the right.
21. Don't forget to leave room for the text and extra room for translation.
22. Keep important images, features, and text away from the margins, and out of the gutter.
23. Give the illustration touchy, feely human elements.
24. Ask a friend, family member, or mentor to review your work.
25. Join a writer's critique group for feedback.

PAGE COUNT

The **page count** is the number of pages in the interior of a book. Most picture books have 32 interior pages, but they can have 24, 28, 32, or more. **Amazon KDP will not bind a** Premium color **children's picture book that has fewer than 24 pages.**

Why are picture books 32 pages? The reason is that 32 is the perfect number of pages for a printer to print on the front and back of one large sheet of paper without wasting paper or using another sheet, saving you and the printer money. Thirty-two pages is also a good book length for young children and their parents to read: not too long and not too short.

You cannot actually use all 32 pages for your story and illustration in a picture book. In a 32-page book, you can only use a maximum of 30 pages or fewer for your story.

At the beginning of the book, there is a **title page**, which displays the book's title, subtitle, author, publisher, and edition. This page is often artistically decorated and is often a duplicate of the cover.

The other page at the beginning of the book is a **copyright page** (called the **front matter**). This page lists the book's publication, legal, copyright, and printing details. You would put the ISBN number on this page, the date of the copyright, the Library of Congress number, if you have one, etc.

If you are publishing a 32-page picture book, but you only have 29 illustrated pages, plus a title and copyright page, then one page will be left blank at the beginning or end of your finished book. If you have 28 illustrated pages, then two pages will be left blank at the end, and so on. Either way, the book will still have 32 pages.

If you are publishing a 28-page book, you will only have 26 pages available for illustration, because you will still lose the title and copyright pages. Browse through a few picture books and see how they are laid out.

LAYING OUT a BOOK

Once the story is written, it's time to plan how the illustration will be laid out. When you **layout** your book, you arrange the text, images, pages, and other objects. Use storyboards to assist you.

Here is an example of using all 32 interior pages of a 32-page picture book. The first two pages are reserved for the title and copyright © pages. Here is an example of how the interior pages would look. You upload every interior page in order and in one PDF file to KDP, beginning with the title and copyright pages.

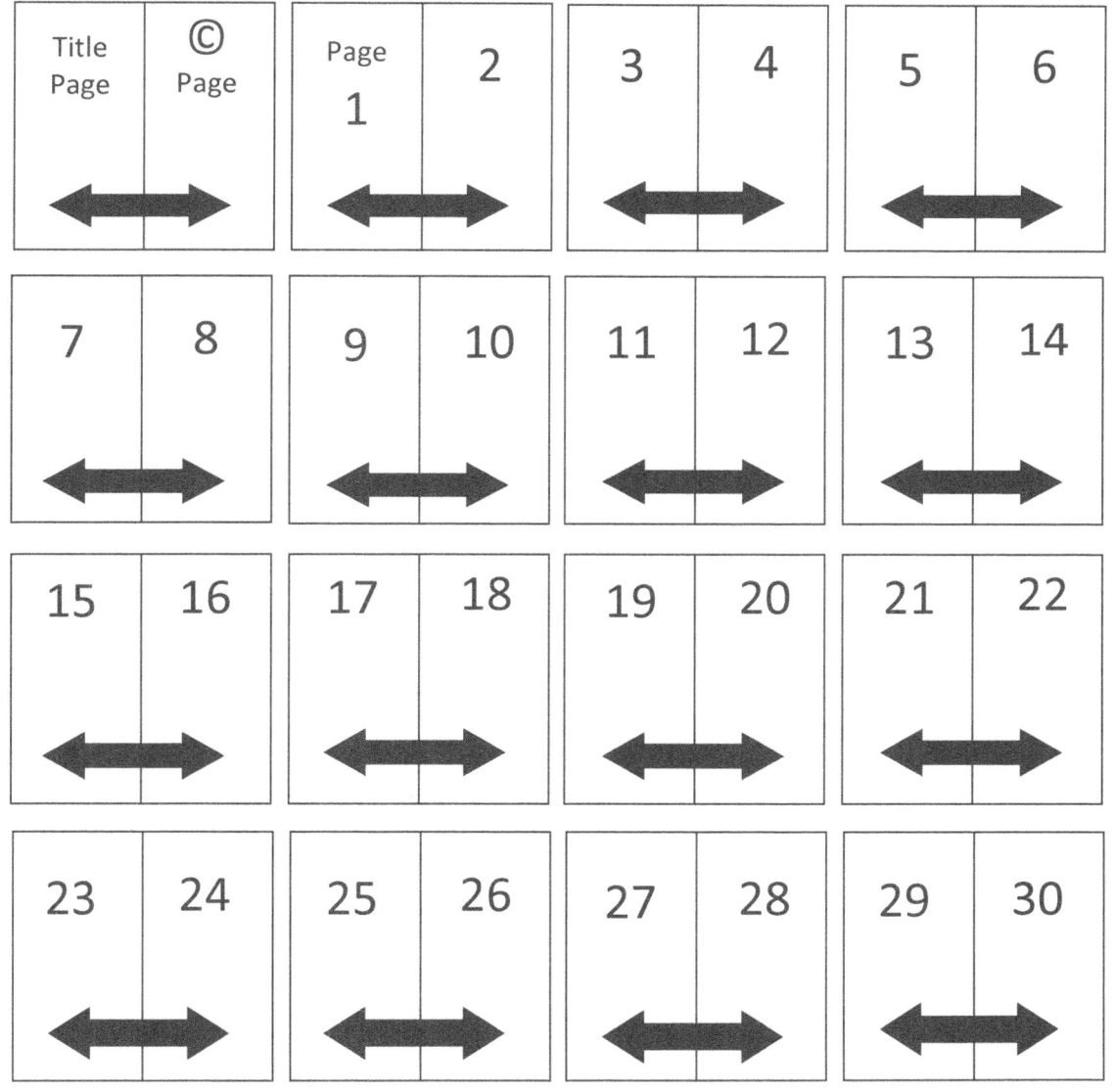

LAYING OUT a BOOK

Here is an example of what the interior page layout of a book will look like if you are only using 28 interior illustrated pages of a 32-page picture book. Again, the first two pages are reserved for the title and copyright © pages. If you are publishing a 32-page picture book and upload 30 interior pages total, including the title page and copyright page in one PDF file, the two extra pages will be left blank when KDP assembles the book. The benefit of publishing a book with extra pages is that you can add content later without having to publish a new book. Put something on those blank pages that you can take off later.

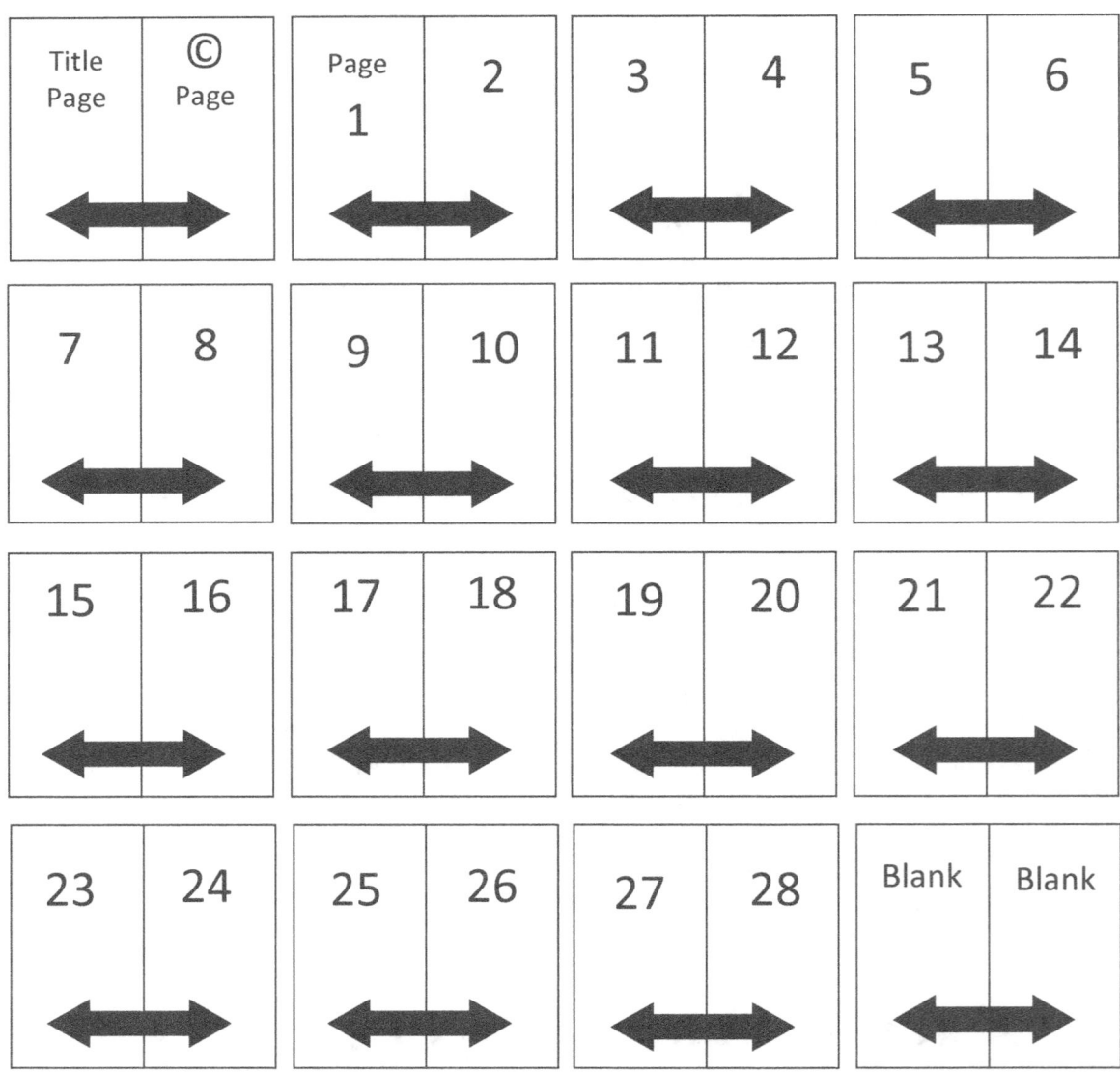

BLANK INTERIOR PAGES

It is perfectly okay to end up with one to four blank pages in your book, but if you're short on content, you can find a creative way to use the extra blank pages, or even add more pages on purpose. Here are some options for making good use of them:

Maze

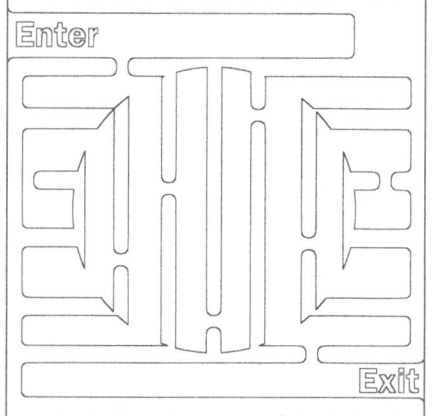

Paper Craft

- lined note pages
- pages with watermarks or decorative elements
- instructions and diagrams
- paper crafts (like origami or a paper plane)
- coloring pages
- mazes and puzzles
- games (crossword, word search, mad libs, etc.)
- images for retelling or restructuring the story
- handmade puppet instructions
- recipes
- a family tree
- a map
- a copy of a news article
- lyrics and/or sheet music
- fast facts about the subject of your story
- details and background information on the topic
- a helpful guide for parents and educators
- resources for more information
- a history lesson
- table of contents
- a glossary of terms

How to make a home-made die.

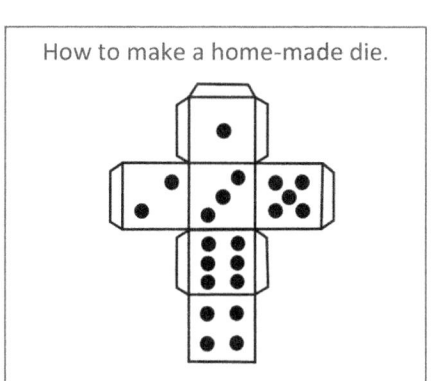

Jumping Jack Paper Puppet

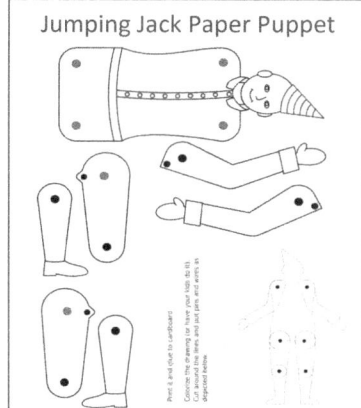

Sheet Music

SET-UP

When you self-publish, you have to prepare your finished story and set up the illustration for uploading to KDP on the computer. **Uploading** is the process of publishing on the Internet. On a self-publishing platform like KDP, your book has to be prepared and uploaded as if it is ready to be pulled from a shelf, with a single cover and back file (spread), and another file with the interior pages in order.

KDP will accept other formats for publishing a downloadable e-book.

1. **Save files as PDFs.** Your cover, spine, and back of the book must be a single PDF. Your interior pages must be a single PDF.

2. **Flatten all transparencies.** Layers can cause files to print with missing, distorted, or discolored content. Consult your software's documentation to learn how.

3. **Embed your fonts.** Incompatible fonts, corrupted fonts, or missing fonts are issues that can easily be avoided by embedding your fonts into your PDFs. When you create a PDF version of your design file, a copy of each necessary font is added to the PDF file itself. Consult your software's documentation to learn how.

4. **Remove crop marks, color bars, and template text.** KDP does not need crop marks or lines that show where pages should be trimmed. Also, remove any template text that might appear, PDF creation guides, or software references.

5. **Ensure your images meet the minimum resolution** of 300 DPI (dots per inch) for professional printing. Images with less than 300 dpi can appear blurry, fuzzy, or pixelated.

6. **Optimize PDFs.** Optimization is useful to reduce your file size, allowing for higher performance when transferring, uploading, viewing, and printing files. Most PDF editing/creation software offers an option called "Fast Web View" or "Optimize," which allows PDF files to display the first few pages of the PDF file when the document is opened, instead of waiting for the full file to be available

7. **Remove file security.** Locked or encrypted files will fail to review.

8. **Check for missing or blank pages.** Manuscripts with missing pages or excessive blank pages will be rejected. A page is blank when there is nothing on the page at all. The page is no longer blank if you add a watermark, decorative swirl, frame, or ruled lines.

UPLOADING the COVER and BACK

If you are self-publishing with Amazon KDP, you upload the cover, spine, and back of the book to the KDP website as a spread, as shown below. KDP will accept a PDF file that is saved at a resolution meant for "High Quality" or "Commercial Press" (300 dpi or higher) printing. Cover files larger than 650MB won't convert. KDP recommends a file size of 40MB or less because files that are too large can slow down printing.

.125" margin + 8" page + spine + 8" page + .125" margin

.125" margin + 10" page + .125" margin

.125 inch margin

.125 inch margin

Spine

You must upload a single PDF file of the spread online with KDP, which includes the back cover, spine, and front as one image.

Set the size of the page spread to include a .125 inch (⅛") margin all around. Plus an additional measurement for the spine, which is determined by the number of interior pages in the book, because the number of interior pages will determine how thick the book will be. KDP offers a template or a calculator online to assist you, but the spine equals the number of pages times .002252. *It's easy if you just search for an online "Book Spine Calculator" or ask AI to calculate for you.

BLEED

The **bleed** is printing that goes beyond the edge of where the pages are trimmed. The bleed ends up being the area that is trimmed off when the pages are cut from the printer's big sheet, and it gives the printer a small amount of leeway for the paper shifting and human error. When adding images, make sure they extend 0.125" (3 mm) past the final trim size on all edges. This will prevent a white border from appearing at the edge and/or out of the gutter when your book is trimmed and bound. If ANY image or graphic extends to the edge on ANY page, even one, then your book has a BLEED.

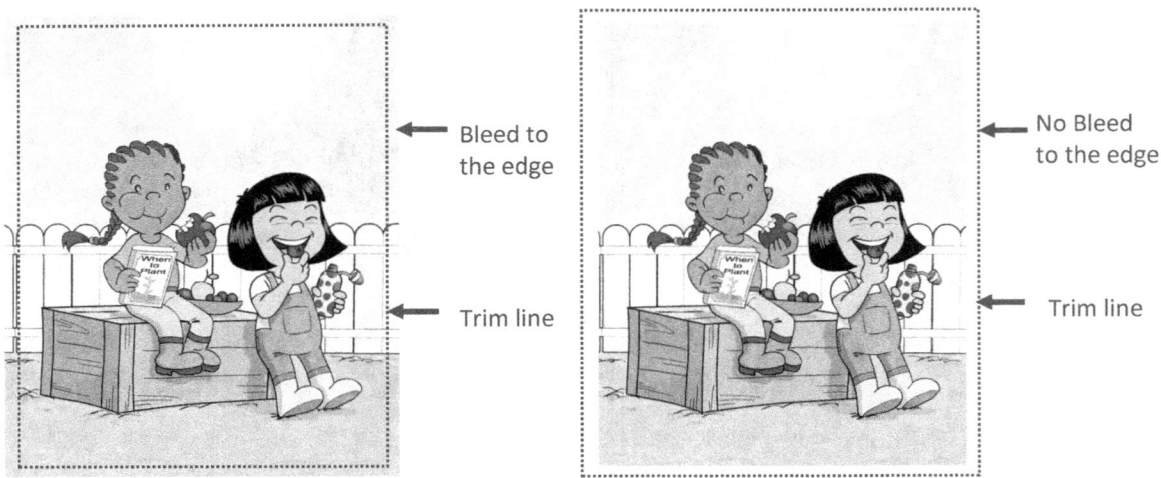

Bleed to the edge

Trim line

No Bleed to the edge

Trim line

If you want to feature **borders** in your book, keep in mind that printers don't always trim evenly. The borders may end up thicker on one side than the other or at a slant. If this happens, the pages will look like they are sitting off-center or sideways. One thick band across the top or bottom yields better results.

Border

Band

The information that appears on the cover of your book has to match the information you enter when you set up the book online with KDP. All of the book's details have to match what the KDP reviewers will see, including the title, subtitle (if you choose to put it on the cover), author's name, illustrator's name, edition, and ISBN. If the information on the cover of your book doesn't match what you type on the online submission form, the book will not pass the review process. This includes the ISBN on the publisher's page inside the book.

PAPERBACK vs. HARDCOVER

Amazon KDP does print hardcover children's picture books. There is a longer wait time for printing and shipping hardcover books, and the shipping will cost more than paperbacks.

Paperback, or softcover books, are books with covers made out of heavy paper stock. They are less expensive to print and lighter to ship than hardcover books. The minimum page count for Premium colored paperbacks is 24. **Hardcover**, or hardback books, have covers made out of heavy cardboard, cloth, or leather, so they last longer, weigh more, cost more to print, and cost more to ship than paperback books. They also take longer to print and assemble than paperbacks, so don't expect to get them quickly. The minimum and maximum page count for their hardcover books is 75 - 550 pages.

BINDINGS

Binding is the act of fastening the individual sheets, or interior pages, of a book together.

Paperback books can be bound in different ways to secure the pages to the spine. **Amazon KDP uses perfect binding**. The pages and cover are glued together at the spine. You can't remove pages that are perfect bound like you can in a loose-leaf binder. The finished paperback books are easy to stack, don't weigh as much as hardback books, and look very professional.

Other popular bindings are available in the paperback printing industry, but not from KDP.

Saddle-stitching is a term that sounds misleading, but it is a method of binding loose-leaf pages of a paperback book using staples down the middle of the gutter. It is an inexpensive way of binding and is commonly seen in Scholastic Book Club books. **KDP <u>does not</u> currently bind this way**.

Perfect Binding

Coil binding is when a single spiraled piece of wire or plastic is wound through holes at the edges of loose-leaf pages. The book is sturdy and looks presentable, but this type of binding can cost more money. It is mostly used for business proposals, school notebooks, or presentations. **KDP does not publish coil-bound books.**

Adhesive casebound is the standard binding option for **hardcover books**. This binding method protects the interior pages with a hardcover. People purchase hardback books if they want to have them for a long time, since the covers are difficult to tear. Expect to pay more for this type of binding and for having two different versions of your book.

If you want to write for babies who don't know any better than to eat the pages of a book, then **board books** are recommended. Board books are unique in that every page is super-thick cardboard that is almost impossible to bend. They are a toy as much as they are a book. The two-page spreads are printed, then cut, assembled, and glued together by hand, one set of pages at a time. **KDP does not currently print board books.**

E-BOOKS

This book focuses on self-publishing a physical printed picture book that a person can hold, rather than a downloadable e-book that can be read on devices such as tablets, phones, and computers from top e-book retailers such as Amazon Kindle, Apple, Barnes & Noble's Nook, and Kobo. Some readers prefer downloaded books, so it's good to publish your book in print as well as downloadable versions. **Amazon KDP only publishes digital books to Kindle** at this time, but there are other services that publish to multiple platforms.

Kindle Kids' Book Creator is a downloadable tool that helps authors create illustrated children's books. The tool has features unique to Kindle devices and helpful apps. For detailed instructions on Kindle Kids' Book Creator, see the user guide. Visit the Kindle Kid's Book Creator product page for more information. With Kindle Kids' Book Creator, you can:

- Add pages and text to imported PDF files.
- Create eBooks with file sizes of up to 650 MB.
- Import illustrations in JPG, PNG, TIFF, and BPP. You can also import and convert PDF files.
- Make changes to books you previously created and published through KDP.
- Preview how your books look on Kindle devices before publishing.

The process of self-publishing an e-book and a print book is slightly different. You will need to take your illustrated manuscript and prepare it for publication differently if you want to publish various downloadable e-book versions.

Though converting your printed picture book to a KDP Kindle e-book is a quick process, it takes a learning curve and some trial and error. A Kindle e-book, like all others, has to be published in a machine-readable format for tablets and e-book readers. Amazon KDP lets you upload and convert your e-book manuscript using several supported file formats, such as WORD docx, HTML, MOBI, ePUB, and others. PDFs do not produce good e-books. KDP encourages you to review your book before you hit the "PUBLISH" button. It is up to you to proofread your book and make sure it looks good on different devices. Another free preview tool is Calibre (https://calibre-ebook.com).

KDP PRINT RUNS

Amazon prints using digital printing, a method of printing that uses a digital-based image, like a PDF, to directly print on the paper stock using high-volume laser or inkjet printers.

A **print run** is the number of copies of a book, magazine, pamphlet, etc., printed at one time. It doesn't matter if you order 12, 200, or 2000 books to be printed. Each time your book is printed, it is one print run. **Amazon KDP identifies each print run with numbers and a barcode on the last page of the book.** If you have quality issues with your POD order, Amazon requests its identifier, which is the barcode on the last page. It identifies the printer and other pertinent information. Check your books immediately, and report any printing issues as soon as possible.

Authors who sell 2,000 or more books, given reasonable deadlines, should consider offset or digital printing with a local printer who specializes in printing books. The same POD print-ready PDF files can always be taken to a local printer that can print 2,000 copies or more. The cost of printing a physical paperback picture book depends mostly on the trim size of the book, the number of interior pages, the paper quality and weight, the binding, color vs. black and white interior pages, and the quantity printed in the print run.

TRADITIONAL PRINT RUNS

Commercial offset printing is an industrial printing process using a printing press with printing plates coated with wet ink. This process produces the highest quality print work and is the most cost-efficient. Multiple pages of the book are printed on one large sheet, then each page is cut to size. Most major publishers print their books using offset printing either in the United States or in a foreign country, like China. **Amazon KDP does not print using offset printers.**

** Printing either way requires cash up front, storage space for the books, and in the case of printing overseas, a two-month printing process followed by 4 to 6 weeks for shipping, if not longer.

TRIM SIZE

The **trim size** of a book is the final size of a printed page after excess edges have been cut off. What size do you want your book to be? Measure the books you enjoy. Commercial printing companies offer standard book sizes, whether you self-publish or not. It's always best to decide on your book's size and **orientation** before you spend time illustrating it and laying it out. Also, keep in mind that the smaller the book, 8.5" x 8.5" vs. 8" x 10", the lighter it is to carry around and the less it costs to ship.

KDP.amazon.com offers the following trim sizes for **portrait**-oriented books. Only the Premium color ink & white paper picture book sizes marked with a ✏ below are eligible for **expanded distribution**.

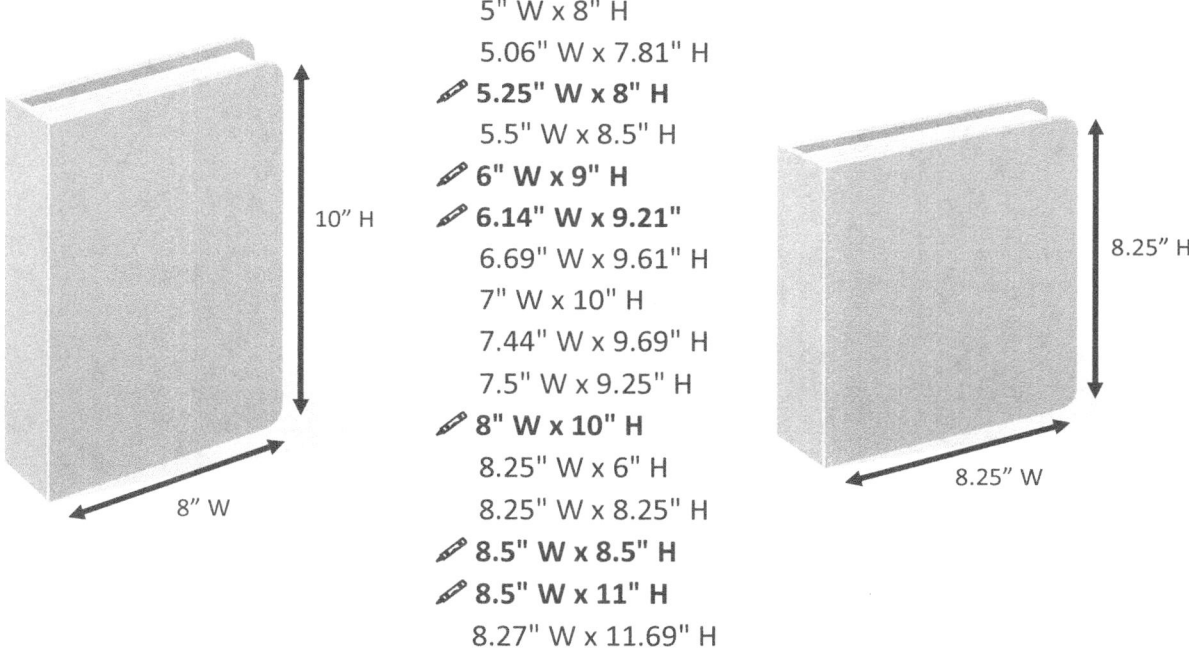

5" W x 8" H
5.06" W x 7.81" H
✏ **5.25" W x 8" H**
5.5" W x 8.5" H
✏ **6" W x 9" H**
✏ **6.14" W x 9.21"**
6.69" W x 9.61" H
7" W x 10" H
7.44" W x 9.69" H
7.5" W x 9.25" H
✏ **8" W x 10" H**
8.25" W x 6" H
8.25" W x 8.25" H
✏ **8.5" W x 8.5" H**
✏ **8.5" W x 11" H**
8.27" W x 11.69" H

10" H

8" W

8.25" H

8.25" W

KDP prints landscape books (wide and short) **with some limitations**. Currently, you can create landscape books with a width up to 8.5 inches and a height between 6 and 11.69 inches. These limitations may have changed since this book was printed.

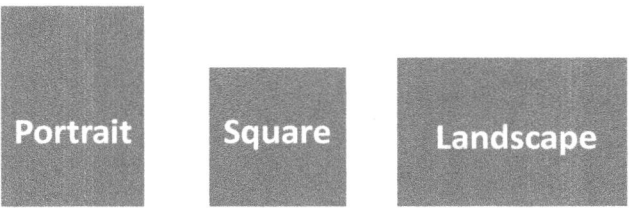

Portrait   Square   Landscape

TRIM SIZE

Authors and illustrators don't want to have images or words cut off when their book goes to the printer, so it's important to know where the printer will trim the pages.

If you are using a template, then there will be crop marks that show you where the paper will be cut. But if you are self-publishing and sizing the book from scratch, know that you will lose .125 inches (⅛ inch) of margin to trimming around each page, so set the margins at .125 inches all around.

To be safe, keep your text and images at least .25 inches (¼ inch) or more from the edge, which combines .125 (⅛ inch) for the trimming and another .125 (⅛ inch) for the safe area. You need to keep all essential illustrations within the **safe area**. This way, you won't lose artwork or text when the book is trimmed.

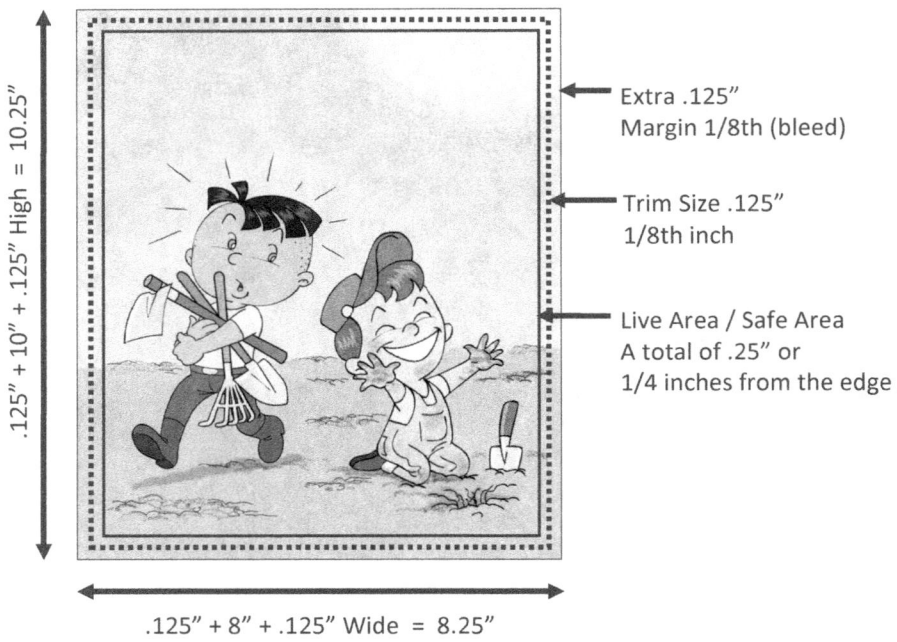

.125" + 10" + .125" High = 10.25"

Extra .125"
Margin 1/8th (bleed)

Trim Size .125"
1/8th inch

Live Area / Safe Area
A total of .25" or
1/4 inches from the edge

.125" + 8" + .125" Wide = 8.25"

Unimportant artwork, like the sky and dirt, can sit in the margin; just know it will most likely be cut off. Using page layout software makes laying out the book easy to measure from page to page, but you can also set page sizes in a program like Microsoft Publisher or Adobe Photoshop. The margins should be set to .25 inches minimum for every page. Above is an example of an 8" W x 10" H self-published page.

Choosing a FONT

A **font** is the STYLE of text printed in a book.

A selection of fonts comes free with whatever writing or design program you use. If you want a specific font and you can't find it for free, you can buy one that is compatible with your writing or design program from an online designer. If you plan to sell your book, you might have to purchase the commercial rights to use the font you like. Some are free for commercial use, and others are not.

Fonts for children's books should be fun, clean, friendly, and simple designs that are easy to read. Look at fonts in popular children's books, and test the font you choose on your friends to see what they think about it.

Here are a few examples of font styles that work for children's books.

Comic Sans   The quick brown fox jumps over the lazy dog.

Century Gothic Pro Reg   The quick brown fox jumps over the lazy dog.

Geo Sans Light   The quick brown fox jumps over the lazy dog.

MV Boli   *The quick brown fox jumps over the lazy dog.*

Unless there is a very good reason to do so, limit your use to one or two font styles at most. Combining multiple fonts and typefaces distracts from the story and makes the book look messy. The first example is over the top, but read the two versions of Sam's story below and see how they make you feel.

Sam **USED TONS OF fonts** in HIS *REPORT*.
They *were cool*,
but now HIS **PAPER** looks messy and **cluttered.**
YIKES!

Sam used tons of fonts in his report.
They were cool,
but now his paper looks messy and cluttered.

YIKES!

Decorative fonts, pops of color, and artistic styles can be used to express emotion, emphasize a sound, or attract the reader's attention. Be consistent and use the same format throughout your book. If you use a decorative font to highlight an expression like "Yikes!" be sure to draw attention to feelings on the other pages in a similar manner.

Fonts with ALL CAPITAL letters, **BOLD** typeface, *script*, *italic*, fancy, old English, stylized, or BUSY designs are a strain on the eyes. Here are some examples of fonts that are just "too much" and might make readers dizzy.

Can you imagine an entire book written with these fonts?

THE QUICK BROWN FOX JUMPS OVER THE LAZY DOG.

The quick brown fox jumps over the lazy dog.

THE QUICK BROWN FOX JUMPS OVER THE LAZY DOG.

The quick brown fox jumps over the lazy dog.

The quick brown fox jumps over the lazy dog.

The quick brown fox jumps over the lazy dog.

THE QUICK BROWN FOX JUMPS OVER THE LAZY DOG.

It is okay to use playful styles, colors, and layouts in your headlines and titles where there are fewer words to read. Again, be consistent. A font you use for a title on one page should be the same font, size, and typeface used for titles on subsequent pages.

Avoid putting too much text on a page. Early readers might find a lot of words to be intimidating, and even adults like to finish the book by bedtime.

Fonts with letters that are tight and very close together are **condensed** and can be difficult to read. When printed, the letters may be indistinguishable from one another.

This font is condensed.

This font is not condensed.

The LETTERS A and G

Young children learn to identify, read, and write the lowercase letter **a** in the infant or single-story style like this... **a.** Instead of "The boy kicked the **ball**," the line should read "The boy kicked the... **ball**." For picture books, it is best to use a font with an infant (single-story) **a**, since preschoolers and school-age children are still learning the letters of the alphabet. Save the two-story **a** for experienced readers.

Another letter that can be confusing to young children is the two-story letter **g** because most children learn to write this style of lowercase **g.** Instead of "The girl balanced the **egg**," the line should read "The girl balanced the... **egg**."

The NUMBER FOUR

Also, pay close attention to how most children learn to write the number four open at the top, like this **4**, instead of closed, like this **4**.

These aren't steadfast rules in the printing world, but school districts may surprise you with the reasons why your book isn't selected for their special programs.

Choosing a TYPEFACE

Typeface refers to a family of fonts of a particular design.

Here are examples of typefaces in the <u>Comic Sans</u> family of fonts. Pick a typeface and stick with it throughout the book. REGULAR works very well in most cases.

Comic Sans (regular) The quick brown fox jumps over the lazy dog.

Comic Sans NARROW The quick brown fox jumps over the lazy dog.

Comic Sans Italic *The quick brown fox jumps over the lazy dog.*

Comic Sans BOLD Italic ***The quick brown fox jumps over the lazy dog.***

Comic Sans BOLD **The quick brown fox jumps over the lazy dog.**

Here are examples of the typeface in the <u>Century Gothic</u> family of fonts.

Century Gothic (regular) The quick brown fox jumps over the lazy dog.

Century Gothic Condensed The quick brown fox jumps over the lazy dog.

Century Gothic Italic *The quick brown fox jumps over the lazy dog.*

Century Gothic Italic BOLD ***The quick brown fox jumps over the lazy dog.***

Century Gothic BOLD **The quick brown fox jumps over the lazy dog.**

Which font do you like?

TEXT COLOR

Black is the most common color of text on the white pages of children's books. Pick a color that will stand out from the background on each page, making it easier to read. Consider placing text in a cloud over a colorful illustration.

It is not recommended, but if you have a black background, then black text obviously won't work. No one will see black on black, so instead use a bright color for the text like white, tan, or yellow.

TEXT SIZE

We read from left to right, following the words, jumping our eyes from the end of one line to the beginning of the next line. To make this process easier on new readers, set the text size larger than what you see in books for adults. A good font size is 14 to 24 points, depending on the font you choose and the age of the reader. Some fonts are designed to be oversized and will look huge without your changing the size.

Leading is the spacing between lines of text. Provide very generous spacing. Most publishers recommend four to six points of space between lines. The bigger the font, the more space there will naturally be between the lines. Many large fonts will naturally increase the space between lines. Four points of space separate each sentence below.

FONT: Comic Sans MS

(14 pt.)   The quick fox jumps over the lazy dog.

(16 pt.)   The quick fox jumps over the lazy dog.

(18 pt.)   The quick fox jumps over the lazy dog.

(20 pt.)   The quick fox jumps over the lazy dog.

TEXT Placement

Text placement refers to where and how the text is placed on the page.

When speaking, we take natural pauses and breaths to express emotion and give listeners a chance to process what we say. Keep line lengths short. Think about natural pauses in speech when placing text in your book. Read the passage below and take a breath at the end of each line. See how the pauses sound and feel.

Once upon a time, there
was a beautiful princess with long flowing
hair. She had a pet green
dragon who breathed fire and let her ride his tail.

The sentences below flow very smoothly because they pause where we naturally take breaths when we talk. The story sounds more dramatic, and the reader is waiting to see what comes next.

Once upon a time,
there was a beautiful princess
with long flowing hair.
She had a pet green dragon
who breathed fire and let her ride his tail.

Keep text away from the center margins and out of the gutter. When the book is bound, words can get cut off.

The two very common arrangements for text placement are:

1. the text is placed strategically within the artwork, such as in open sky, empty space, or areas with low detail.

2. the text appears underneath the artwork, often centered or aligned left.

TITLE and SUBTITLE

The **title** is a name or phrase that identifies or describes a book. **Enter the title EXACTLY as it appears on the cover of your book, word for word.** The title should be short, intriguing, thought-provoking, and to the point. Brainstorm titles by writing down themes, keywords, idioms, catchphrases, rhyming words, and every word or expression that would help readers predict the subject of your book. Arrange these in different combinations. Try summarizing your work in one sentence, then reducing that sentence down to a phrase. A title doesn't have to read like a perfect sentence. A misleading, unclear, or vague title is a missed opportunity to capture a buyer's attention and a great reason for poor reviews.

- Aim the title toward your audience.
- Keep your title short, simple, and to the point.
- Study titles in your genre that have caught your attention.
- Write the title in the primary language of your book.
- Google the topic of your story for inspiration.
- Type the description into AI and ask for a title.
- Test your title on friends and family.

A **subtitle** is an optional secondary title that contains additional information about the book. But a subtitle is especially important for an unknown author looking to get their book found on Amazon. Many cute titles just don't explain what the book is about. This is where the subtitle comes in handy. It should be a short, very concrete supplemental description with additional information and more detail about the content of your book. **You don't have to enter a subtitle on KDP, and if you do enter a subtitle, it does not have to appear printed on the cover of your book.**

Without subtitles, no one would know what these two books were actually about.

1. **Title:** *We Eat Food That's Fresh*
   Subtitle: *A Children's Picture Book about Tasting New Foods (Multicultural)*

   Appears like this on Amazon KDP:
   We Eat Food That's Fresh: A Children's Picture Book about Tasting New Foods (Multicultural)

2. Title: *We Love the Company*

    Subtitle: *A Children's Picture Book about Table Manners (Multicultural)*

    Appears like this on Amazon KDP:

    We Love the Company: A Children's Picture Book about Table Manners (Multicultural)

KDP will place the colon between the title and subtitle. Together, **your title and subtitle must be 200 characters or fewer, and you cannot change the title or subtitle after your book is published on KDP.**

Be sure not to add anything from the following list of prohibited items in the title & subtitle fields:

- Unauthorized references to other titles or authors
- Unauthorized references to a trademarked term.
  Look for these symbols, ^{TM} or $^{\circledR}$
- References to sales ranks, such as "top-selling, "chart-topping," or "bestselling"
- References to advertisements or promotions, such as "Free" or "BOGO"
- Punctuation with no words, such as "!!!!!!!!" or "??????"
- Repeating generic keywords like "notebook," "books," "journal," "gifts," etc.

DESCRIPTION

The **description** is a short statement or paragraph that explains the subject or topic of a book. It appears on the DETAILS page of Amazon.com, along with an image of the book's cover. After the title and cover, the description is the most important part of marketing your book.

Carefully select words that express the meaning of your story, and keep revising the description as you think of ways to improve it further. You can always go back and add to or change the description on your details page later.

Because your book description will show on the Amazon website, it can include formats such as line breaks, italicized fonts, and bold text using **Hypertext Markup Language (HTML).** Amazon provides a guide and examples on how to type a description with HTML in their online tutorial.

Here are some tips for writing a description:

- Hook the audience with the first sentence so they will continue reading.
- Write a compelling answer to the question, "Why should someone read this book?"
- Summarize the story without giving away its secrets.
- Stay on point. Avoid overwhelming the reader with useless details.
- Write descriptions that capture the essence of the genre. If you have written a mystery, then make the description mysterious. If your book is playful, then write a lighthearted, amusing description.
- Read descriptions of similar books for inspiration.
- Avoid explaining the subject. If your story is about a child who ate vegetables, don't explain what vegetables are, or why children should eat them. Tell the reader about your story.
- For nonfiction or educational books, include the benefits of reading the book and specifically what the reader will learn.
- Include other helpful information. What lesson does the story teach? What's the moral of the story? What educational domain or foundation does the story address? What concepts are being presented?

Amazon KDP has book **description restrictions** and will not accept any of the following information in the description:

- Phone numbers, physical mail addresses, email addresses, or website URLs
- Reviews, quotes, testimonials, or requests for the same
- Advertisements, watermarks on images, or promotional material
- Time-sensitive information: promotional tours, seminars/workshops, or lecture dates
- Availability, price, alternative ordering information, like links to other websites
- Spoiler information for Books, Music, Video, or DVD (BMVD) listings
- Any keywords or copyright book tags/phrases: *The Wizard of Oz,* "There's no place like home." — or *Ghostbusters,* "Who you gonna call?"
- Unicode emojis

TITLE PAGE and COPYRIGHT PAGE

The **title page** is the first interior page of the book. It announces the title, subtitle, author, illustrator, and publisher of the book. Illustrations are also common on title pages. They can mirror the artwork on the cover or be more decorative, as you see here.

COVER

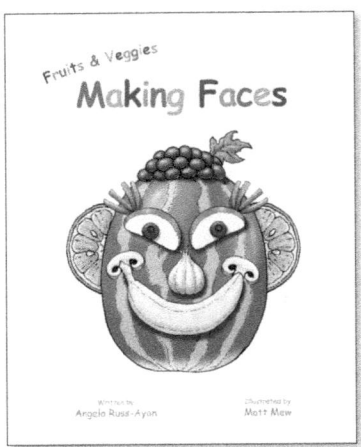

TITLE PAGE

The **copyright page** is where you print important information about the book, which is usually found on the back side (verso) of the title page at the beginning of the book. This page tells the reader who owns the original work of authorship. No part of the story goes on the title or copyright pages.

As soon as you create your original work, you automatically have a copyright, which prevents others from copying, publishing, or performing your work without your permission. A copyright protects the words in your book.

It's important to know that you may not own the copyright of a book you wrote as an employee of a company/school, or if someone paid you to write the book under a work-for-hire contract. Check your contractual obligations.

You don't have to print all of the information listed below on the **copyright page**, but the information below is pretty much standard for every book:

- ☐ The copyright notice - owner of the copyright.
- ☐ The year the book was published.
- ☐ The reservation of rights. Example: *All rights reserved.*
- ☐ The publisher's logo, name, and address or website.
- ☐ The ISBN (International Standard Book Number).

Open a published book for any age and see what is printed on the Copyright Page.

Also, copyright registration is voluntary through the U. S. Copyright Office. Doing so gives you specific legal advantages and protects you against copycats. Here is the link for more information: https://www.copyright.gov

COPYRIGHT NOTICE
and
RESERVATION RIGHTS

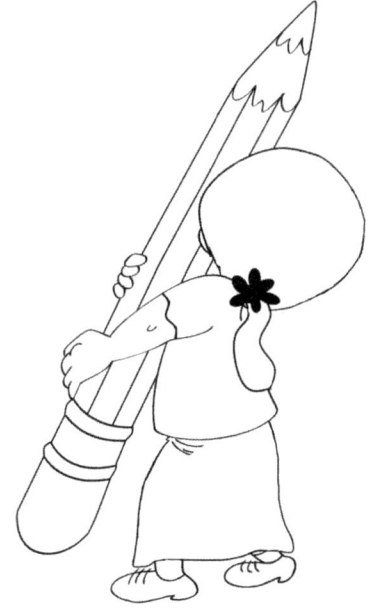

You'll want to declare to readers that you own the rights to your work or story with a copyright notice. The job of the copyright notice is to tell the reader that you are the person who wrote the words or story, and you are the owner of the copyright. The notice can be written in one of these three ways.

Copyright © Anthony Hall, 2019. All Rights Reserved.
Copyright © 2019 Anthony Hall. All Rights Reserved.
Copyright © 2019 by Anthony Hall. All Rights Reserved.

The copyright consists of four components:

- **"Copyright":** Your book may be published in other countries, so you may want to spell out the word "copyright" before the symbol, so there is no confusion.
- **©:** This is the universal symbol for copyright in the United States and most countries.
- **Copyright owner's name:** This would be the creator's name, but it is okay to use a pen name or pseudonym.
- **Year of publication:** This is the year you publish the story, not the year you first created the story or got the idea for it.

Additional information that can be printed on the copyright page:

- Where the book was printed (City, State, Country).

- The **Library of Congress Number** or **Pre-assigned Control Number (PCN)** is a unique number assigned to a book. Librarians use it to find your book in the national databases. You can print your book without it and add it later. It usually only takes one or two days to be assigned. Here is the link to more information. **A Library of Congress Number is not required for publishing on KDP.**

  https://www.loc.gov/publish/pcn/

- **Cataloging-in-Publication Data (CIP).** The purpose of the CIP data is to make it easier for libraries to purchase and circulate the book. Without CIP data, librarians have to do the work themselves to determine what the book is about and assign classification numbers. **The CIP block is not required for publishing on KDP.**

  CIP data is specific to the book it catalogs; you cannot reuse the CIP data block you used on other titles or editions of your book. Nor can you use someone else's CIP data. You get the CIP block either from the Library of Congress or from another source for a fee - usually before the book is published.

If you publish through Amazon KDP, **you can always add details to your copyright page later.**

Here is additional information that can be printed on the copyright page:

- The edition of the book (1st edition, 2nd edition, etc.).
- Numbers, dates, or images to identify the version of your book that was printed. Change this information on each upload of the interior copyright page. If there is a problem with the printing, ask the customer to provide your identifier. Amazon identifies each print run using a barcode on the last page of each book.
- Contact information for the author and illustrator.
- Short biographies of the author and illustrator.
- A list of other books the author has published. This is a chance to promote other books you have written. If someone likes your book, they might look for others you have published.
- Some publishers use the copyright page to give credit to special contributors to the book, like designers, proofreaders, and copyeditors.

When you create your copyright page, pick the information that seems most suitable and relevant to your book.

Here is a sample of a copyright page in a book. The copyright notice and ISBN have to appear on the copyright page, no matter what.

INTERNATIONAL STANDARD BOOK NUMBER (ISBN)

The **International Standard Book Number** (ISBN) is a unique number assigned to each edition of a printed book. If you want your printed book on shelves in either bookstores or libraries, you'll need an ISBN. The ISBN is what retail stores and libraries use to keep track of books. ISBNs allow for efficient marketing and distribution of books because they are the global standard for book identification. Most retailers require an ISBN on every book sold.

If you see a book you like, and you want to buy a copy for yourself, all you need is the ISBN to find the same book in a bookstore or online, because one ISBN matches only one published book. You cannot use the same ISBN on different books or different versions of books. **KDP will provide you with a free ISBN to publish your paperback book.**

An ISBN links to essential information about your book and identifies:

- the specific title, edition, and author
- the country or language of the book
- the publisher of the book
- the format and physical properties (binding, size, number of pages, etc.)
- identifies a book's specific format, edition, and publisher

You can find the **ISBN** along with the **barcode** on the lower right corner of the back of a printed book, and again on the copyright page. All physical copies have ISBNs assigned.

None of the top **eBook** retailers, such as Amazon, Apple, Barnes & Noble, or Kobo requires an ISBN for electronic books, but some authors assign one to every version of their books as a way of keeping track of what they've published. It's interesting to note that many bestselling Kindle books on Amazon don't have ISBNs assigned.

ISBN

Every ISBN has 13 digits. Up until January 1, 2007, ISBNs only had ten numbers, so some books have both 10 and 13-digit ISBNs. Here is an example of the ISBN for the 32-page, perfect-bound, paperback version of a book entitled *Fruits and Veggies Row by Row*. Try entering this number in a Google search without the dashes to see what comes up.

ISBN 13: 9781958627051

Once an ISBN is assigned to your paperback and the book is published on KDP, you can't change the author's name, book's binding, the size of the book, or the number of pages, but you can publish a new version of the book with a new ISBN. If you have a hardback and a paperback version of a book, you have to have two different ISBNs. If one book has 32 pages, and the other has 100, you have to have two different ISBNs. If two books are two different sizes, you have to have two different ISBNs. If one book is in color and the other is black and white, you will need two different ISBNs. If you change the name of the book after it is published, you will need to acquire a new ISBN for the new title and republish it. You can change the cover design, words, and illustration on the interior pages, the price, and the description of the book, without having to change the ISBN.

Limited- or low-content books, such as journals and notebooks, are no longer assigned a free ISBN number by KDP. They are published with an assigned Amazon ASIN number. Limited content books are also not allowed expanded distribution, and will not be given a "Look Inside" option on the Amazon detail page. Since there is limited content, there won't be much to look at anyway.

You don't have to buy an ISBN for your book when you publish with KDP, but some authors purchase a block of ISBNs because they want their trade or company name to be associated with every book they publish. The United States ISBN Agency is the only agency authorized to assign ISBNs to publishers in the United States, U.S. Virgin Islands, Guam, and Puerto Rico. You can purchase ISBNs in blocks of 10, 100, and 1000. KDP authors are allowed to buy one ISBN or a batch of ISBNs at a discounted rate from Bowker. Here is the link to more information for purchasing ISBNs by Bowker:

https://www.isbn.org

BARCODE

A **barcode** is a series of printed lines of varying widths that can be read by an optical scanner. It is different from an ISBN. Lines and bars on a barcode make it easier for retail stores and distributors to identify your book by scanning the bars (or lines) with an electronic tool, instead of typing all 13 numbers of the ISBN. Retail stores use barcodes to keep track of inventory, sell books at the cash register, and avoid human error. If sellers had to type thirteen numbers into the register every time a customer purchased a book, there would definitely be a lot of human error. The barcode above is pretty standard, but barcodes can have different looks to them.

The barcode identifies:
- the ISBN number
- the type of money or currency in which the book is being sold
- the price of the book

Can you find the $16.99 price in the sample barcode above? The "5" before the price indicates that you will be paying in U.S. currency.

You don't automatically get a barcode when you buy an ISBN, but whether you buy an ISBN or get one free from KDP, **KDP will generate a barcode for you based on the ISBN**. All you have to do is leave space for a 2" by 1.2" white box in the lower right-hand corner of the book's back cover. If you put text or artwork in that space, it will get covered up by the barcode that is placed there.

If you want to place your own barcode on the back of the book to match your ISBN, there is a box you check to let KDP know.

PROOFREADING Your BOOK

Proofreading is finding and correcting mistakes in a story before the final copies are printed. We all make mistakes. The good thing is that we can always correct them. Here are some problems to watch out for when you **launch the previewer** in "Edit Paperback Content" from the BOOKSHELF and after you have received a physical proof of your book:

◊ Make sure you spelled your book title, subtitle, name, and contributors' names correctly on the book and the KDP Paperback Details page.
◊ Double-check the ISBN and other information on the interior copyright page.
◊ Confirm that the ISBN on the barcode matches the one on your copyright page.
◊ Make sure the barcode that KDP places on the back doesn't cover important images or text.
◊ Make sure the text and images are not too close to the edge, over the margin, or in the gutter.
◊ Check for missing or cut-off text on all pages.
◊ Confirm that the text is all in the same font, style, and size.
◊ Look at your book in the spread view and make sure your text and graphics line up on the left and right pages.
◊ Watch all images that might be low-resolution (blurry and fuzzy), or stretched and distorted. Cut off or remove parts of the image that might distract the reader.
◊ Make sure your colors are CMYK, not RGB.
◊ Make sure your images are flattened, not layered.
◊ Check if your images and pages are formatted the same: with or without borders, shadows, custom frames, consistent spacing and margins, consistent fonts and sizes of titles, etc.
◊ If required, make sure all lists are in numerical, alphabetical order, or dated order.
◊ If you referred to something in your book, such as a diagram, chart, or page, make sure the reference numbers, letters, or page numbers match up.
◊ Check for unusual and uneven line spacing.
◊ Double-check grammar, spelling, and punctuation.
◊ Do all of the paragraphs begin the same, with or without indentations or fancy letters?
◊ Look for missing pages.
◊ Check that the pages are in order.
◊ Pages don't need to be numbered, but if they are, are they numbered correctly?
◊ Check to see that your table of contents and/or glossary page numbers are correct.

OPENING an ACCOUNT
with Amazon KDP

https://kdp.amazon.com

The first thing you have to do in order to self-publish is open an account on Amazon KDP. This includes entering payment, banking, and tax information. Opening a KDP account also opens an Amazon.com account using the same login information. This is the account through which you will order your author copies.

Read the terms and conditions carefully before agreeing to them. You can only enter one email address and one phone number, and **you are not allowed to open more than one account with KDP** using the same social security number or EIN (Business Tax ID Number). To do so will result in Amazon closing your account without notice, removing your books from their platform, and banning you from KDP for life.

Other infractions that will close an account are copyright infringement and not following content guidelines. **Just because you see a book selling on Amazon.com doesn't mean it's okay to sell a similar book.** In six months, that book probably won't be there. The KDP review team doesn't catch every issue when your book is published, and it takes a while for Amazon's bots to find infractions and shut down accounts.

If you apply for a small business EIN from the American Internal Revenue Service (IRS) after you open your account, you can log in and update your payment information.

There are three ways to get paid royalties:
- **Direct Deposit:** Amazon automatically deposits into your bank account. Direct deposits are cheaper and slower than wire transfers.
- **Wire Transfer:** an electronic payment service for transferring funds by wire in single (generally large) payments to another person or institution.
- **Check** in the mail.

Direct deposit is the preferred method for most authors. You will receive email notifications when funds are deposited into your account.

UPLOADING Your BOOK to KDP

To upload your book, you have to use a computer and **open an account with Amazon KDP**. Children may need their parents to help enter some of the required information.

https://kdp.amazon.com

You need to have the following:

- a hi-resolution PDF spread of your book (cover and back).
- a hi-resolution PDF of the individual interior pages, which includes the title page and the copyright page.
- an accurate, attention-grabbing description of your book.
- keywords that describe and help buyers find your book.
- an idea of the category for your book. KDP provides both *juvenile fiction* and *juvenile non-fiction* categories from which to choose.
- an idea of what the price of your book will be. Browse through Amazon.com for similar books to get an idea of how to price yours.

The KDP system will not allow you to publish a book that has glaring errors, like improperly sized pages, text that falls outside of the margin, mismatched titles, duplicate ISBN numbers, text that falls outside of the margins, and will display ERRORS on the left margin. Keep in mind that the KDP system and reviewers don't catch everything. They have no personal interest in your book. It is up to you to proofread and find any problems.

Don't be surprised if you need to upload revised versions of your book's cover and interior files multiple times before you get it right. It's pretty normal for the book to get **rejected** for some reason. Even after your book is published, you can resubmit your files and make some changes, but when your book goes live on Amazon, anyone can purchase the live version until you make your revisions.

After your book is published, KDP will contact you with a "quality warning" if readers report problems with your book. It should not come to that, so put your best work out there because you don't want bad reviews on your detail page.

LOG IN to your account on **https://kdp.amazon.com**

KDP will step you through all of the questions in the order below.
But keep in mind that KDP may have reformatted their publishing pages
since the publishing of this book.

❋ PAPERBACK DETAILS ❋

1. Begin at the **BOOKSHELF** on the upper left side of the KDP page.
2. Select **+ CREATE** and select **CREATE PAPERBACK** and answer the questions as they appear.
3. Choose your paperback's **PRIMARY LANGUAGE**.
4. Enter your book's **TITLE** as it appears on the book's cover.
5. Enter your book's **SUBTITLE**. It is not required, and if you have one, it does not have to appear on the cover of the book. The subtitle is used as an extension of the title to explain, describe, or clarify the title or book's topic. On KDP, the subtitle will appear as a continuation of the title, separated by a colon (:). You will not need to place the colon.
6. Enter your book's **SERIES** information. Here is an example from the *Lord of the Rings* series of books:
   Series name: *The Fellowship of the Ring*
   Series number: 1
7. Enter the **EDITION** number, if this is one of multiple versions of your book.
8. Enter the full **AUTHOR's NAME**.
9. Add any **CONTRIBUTORS** one at a time. (Illustrator, translator, editor, etc.)
10. Enter your book's **DESCRIPTION**. KDP limits the number of characters to 4000.
11. Enter up to eight **KEYWORDS** or popular search phrases. (limited characters)
12. Choose up to two browsing **CATEGORIES**. (Fiction or nonfiction, and sub-categories)
13. Indicate whether your book is a **LOW/LIMITED-CONTENT** book with minimal or no content on the interior pages, such as a journal, notebook, or sketchbook. Low or limited content books are no longer assigned an ISBN number. They are given an ASIN number by KDP and are not allowed expanded distribution.
14. Indicate whether your book is a **LARGE PRINT** book with a font size over 16 pts.
15. Enter whether there is **ADULT CONTENT** in your book. Yes or no? There normally wouldn't be, since you have written a children's picture book.
16. **SAVE** your entries.

❋ PAPERBACK CONTENT ❋

17. Select whether you want KDP to assign an **ISBN** or whether you wish to enter one you purchased from Bowker, enter the company or trade name to which the purchased ISBN is linked.

18. Enter the **PUBLICATION DATE** for your book. If you don't enter a date, KDP will use the date your book goes live on Amazon.com.

19. Select your **PRINT OPTIONS**.
    - ⇒ Premium color interior pages with white paper. (This is the most common.)
    - ⇒ Black and white with cream interior pages. (Not used for picture books)
    - ⇒ Black and white with white interior pages. (Not used for picture books)

20. Select which **TRIM SIZE** you would like your book to be. What are the dimensions (width and height) of your book? You will have set the dimensions of your book in the design program you used.

21. Indicate whether there is a **BLEED** (artwork all the way to the edge of the pages), or no bleed. If there is just one page with artwork to the edges, select bleed.

22. Select a **FINISH** for the cover. Matte or glossy? (Glossy is most common.)

23. Upload your **MANUSCRIPT** as one formatted PDF file. You can also upload a DOC (.doc), DOCX (.docx), HTML (.html), or RTF (.rtf).

24. Upload the spread of the **COVER AND BACK** as one PDF. Design your own cover or create a cover using KDP's Cover Creator tool. KDP has commercial-free stock images you can use.

25. Check the box if you are providing your own **BARCODE,** or Amazon will place the barcode on the back of your book.

26. Preview your cover and interior pages to check for any formatting issues by clicking on **LAUNCH PREVIEWER**. You won't be able to move on to the next page until you do. The previewer takes a few minutes to load and will allow you to flip through your

book from cover to back page by page, as if you were holding it in your hands. The pages will be viewed in low resolution.

The previewer will also display identifiable **ERRORS** on the left side of the page, along with the page numbers where the errors occur. Clicking on the page numbers in the ERROR section will take you to the pages with the problems.

Most common file rejections are the result of text and images over the margins, bleed when you marked "no bleed," embedded fonts, or an incorrect ISBN number on the publisher page. KDP reviewers are not checking for grammatical errors, low-resolution images, issues with your illustration, or problems with your story. Such issues are not their responsibility.

You have to launch the previewer and check the layout of your book <u>every time you make a change</u> to its cover or interior pages.

Turn the pages of your ONLINE preview book and check each page. Click **"Exit Print Previewer"** on the lower right side to correct the errors. You will not be able to "Approve" the layout until the errors are corrected and either the cover or interior pages are uploaded again. Upload your cover or interior files again and again until you are happy with the layout and have no errors. It helps if you date your revisions so you know which files have been uploaded at a glance.

** Review the **SUMMARY** that appears at the bottom of the page after you have previewed your book. Make sure the information matches what you entered.

27. Click **SAVE** and **CONTINUE**.

❋ PAPERBACK RIGHTS and PRICING ❋

28. Select the **TERRITORIES** for which you hold distribution rights. Worldwide or select countries? If this is your original work, you hold worldwide rights.

29. The primary marketplace for the United States is Amazon.com. The **LIST PRICE** is the retail price you want the book to sell for on Amazon.com. It is the price the public will see on Amazon's detail page. KDP displays the minimum and maximum retail price it will allow. It will also display your **PRINTING COST** and the **ROYALTY** they will pay per region under "other marketplaces."

30. Select **EXPANDED DISTRIBUTION** if you want to reach more readers by distributing your paperback through bookstores, online retailers, libraries, and academic institutions. You don't have to select this option when you first upload. You can select it later. You will require a separate ISBN if you plan on self-publishing the same book with expanded distribution on another platform, such as IngramSpark, unless you have purchased an ISBN for your book.

31. Click to order and pay for one to five **PROOF COPIES** of your book, which you can purchase through your Amazon shopping cart. The proofs come with a gray **watermark** across the middle of the cover that says "Not for Resale." It is standard in the Industry. Proofs are for reviewing your work and sending your book to professional reviewers who are not supposed to sell your book.

At this point, you can save your book as a **DRAFT** and continue to make changes either now or later, or **PUBLISH YOUR PAPERBACK BOOK**.

After you hit PUBLISH, your book is reviewed to ensure it meets KDP's detail, content, and quality standards. Until then, the book's status will be "**In Review**" on your **BOOKSHELF**. When it passes the review, it will appear as "**LIVE**" on your **BOOKSHELF**. You will be contacted by email whether your book does or does not pass KDP's review.

It can take up to 72 hours (or more) for your book to be available for purchase on Amazon, and even longer during the holidays. It can take up to five days for other marketplaces to show as "in stock." It can take 24-48 hours for the book's description to appear on the detail page, and 10 days for the "Look Inside" feature to appear on your Amazon detail page.

You will receive an email from Kindle Direct Publishing when your book is published that says, **"Your paperback book has been published!"**

PROMOTING Your BOOK

If no one knows about your book, you probably won't sell very many. You have to promote and actively support it in the marketplace. Write an excellent description and type the right keywords on KDP's detail page to help people find your book. **Keywords** are words and short phrases that define the subject of your book. Thousands of people type keywords into search engines like Google.com to find books every day. For example, a mother might search using the keyword phrase "picture book about going to the doctor" on Amazon.com or Google.com to find a book for her child. Look for other creative ways to promote and **publicize** your book to make it widely known. Here are a few suggestions, some of which you can do before you publish.

- Invite friends and family for a reading at home or a local venue, like a coffee shop, pizza restaurant, or private club.
- Offer to read your book at bookstores, book fairs, libraries, and special events.
- Share the most up-to-date information about yourself and your work/s with millions of readers on Amazon's Author Central and other literary sites.
- Build a website for your book and authorship.
- Write multiple articles and blogs about the subject of your book and link them to your promotional page.
- Establish a social media presence with posts, images, videos, and quotes. Create unique, attention-grabbing posts that relate to your book.
- Send e-mailer blasts to potential customers.

- Submit your book for reviews and literary awards. Promote positive reviews and awards on the book's KDP description, social media posts, press releases, and emailers.
- Read your book live on video for sites like YouTube. People who buy in bulk want to read the entire book first.
- Present your knowledge of the book's topic in workshops or training sessions. Then send emails to attendees offering a discount on a printed or eBook version.
- Hold raffles and free giveaways, featuring your book, for groups and attendees interested in your topic.
- Solicit schools for author visits and distribute order forms to students.
- Submit your book to school supply and specialty catalogs. They often build kits around specific topics such as science, physical fitness, nutrition, math, etc.
- Send promotional copies to professionals, grant writers, and nonprofits who are in a position to buy.
- Inform local newspapers, online bloggers, radio stations, and talk show hosts about your book.
- Connect your story to trending topics and current news.
- Connect your story to niche markets and address those market needs.
- Distribute promotional items like bookmarks, postcards, or coloring pages.
- Release an e-Book, audiobook, or companion book such as a coloring book, puzzle book, or journal.
- Purchase internet advertising to promote your book.
- You've done most of the work. Now, publish your book in other languages.
- Take polls. Start an online discussion or debate about the subject of your book.

CHALLENGES with AMAZON KDP
The Forum
www.kdpcommunity.com

Publishing with Amazon KDP isn't always rosy. If you are ordering author copies from KDP to dropship books directly to a customer, you will not be able to quality check the books first. Ask the customer to open a few books in each shipping box and flip through them for a spot check. KDP will refund authors and customers for substandard books, but issues must be reported within a designated time.

In your Amazon.com description, state that your books are printed on demand and that any quality issues should be reported to you as the author immediately, so customer complaints can be addressed asap. This is why it's important to build a website where people can find you using your author name, book title, or ISBN.

- **Appearance -** Remember, a proof isn't printed on the same equipment as an Amazon printed book order. Occasionally, order your book directly from Amazon as if you were a customer, to ensure the quality is still the same.

- **Receive two different books in one order -** If there are returns on Amazon's storage shelf, customers may receive two different versions of your book: the old version and the most recent or updated version.

- **Split shipments -** When ordering multiple books of the same title, they are often shipped in separate packages in varying quantities. For example, when ordering 30 books, the customer may receive 29 books in one box and one in another, or 20 books in one box and 10 in another.

- **Printing issues - KDP can't guarantee perfectly positioned and trimmed books.** Books may be assembled with interior pages out of order. Pages may be sitting sideways, improperly aligned, or cropped past the bleed (causing 2mm white strips to either extend out of the gutter or along the edges of the pages).

- **Color issues -** Colors are not true. Make sure images are flattened, and remember to upload/submit the images in RGB color mode. Also, black is rarely true black.

- **Lack of communication with the printers -** KDP printers do not work with clients directly to advise them about design issues or answer questions about printing. Authors can use the forum or contact Amazon KDP directly with inquiries.

STORYBOARD

Use this template to plan out your book by drawing rough sketches and writing brief descriptions. Enter page numbers in the circles. Copy these pages as needed.

STORYBOARD

STORYBOARD

STORYBOARD

How to Self-Publish a Children's Picture Book   www.AbridgeClub.com

STORYBOARD

TRADITIONAL PUBLISHING HOUSES

Self-publishing has become very popular, but we can't talk about self-publishing without talking about publishing the traditional way. **Amazon KDP is not a traditional publishing house.** If you are self-publishing, you don't have to worry about the traditional side of the publishing industry, but it is worth informing you about just the same.

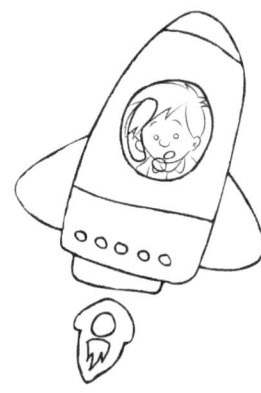

A **traditional publishing house** is a professional company that specializes in publishing books. This type of publisher has the money, connections, and influence to launch a successful book and reach a wide audience. Even publishers with a stellar reputation publish around four children's books a year, but they don't publish just any book. It is also extremely rare for a publisher or agent to consider publishing a book that an author has already self-published using KDP or any other service because publishers want the **first rights** to offer a book to the public. Publishing houses want to launch books that are fresh, new, and relevant, not books that have already been released digitally or in print. Unless, of course, it is a self-published popular mega-seller with a track record that is guaranteed to make them money.

Manuscripts are submitted typed or electronically to a traditional publisher, depending on their **submission** guidelines.

When a manuscript is submitted to a traditional publishing house by an author, an editor reviews the book and decides whether to offer the writer a deal for the rights to print the book or reject it. If a manuscript is submitted without an agent, it is considered unsolicited. An **unsolicited** manuscript was not requested by the publisher and may not be considered without first sending the publisher a query (one-page letter) to see if they are interested in reading it.

Even though every manuscript has the potential to be chosen, many come from very experienced authors or have been recommended by literary agents. The review process at a traditional publishing house can take anywhere from three to six months, depending on the size of the company, but some authors have received responses as late as 12 months after they've submitted. Traditional publishing houses receive hundreds of books each month. When they offer an author a deal, the deal is based on how well the editor thinks the author's book will sell. In exchange for the rights to publish and sell the book, the publishing house pays the author an advance on future royalties.

Many traditional publishing houses have particular specialties which encompass children's books, novels, coloring books, puzzle books, comic books, travel books, cookbooks, magazines, or any combination.

A traditional publisher also specializes in genres. A **genre** is a particular category of book, like science fiction, thriller, horror, comedy, action and adventure, romance, autobiography, and so on. Within their genres, they might get even more specific and only sell *young adult* science fiction, *baby* board books, or *vegan* cookbooks.

Traditional publishers have specific **guidelines for submissions** and a website where authors can gather more information. Another resource worth adding to your library is a book called **The Writer's Market**, which is updated and published every year to help authors and illustrators navigate the publishing industry. It includes updated contacts, submission information, and listings for book publishers, consumer magazines, trade magazines, contests, and literary awards.

What do traditional publishing houses do?

They have a staff of professionally trained employees. Depending on the size, they do a lot.

- Pay the author an advance and future royalties for the book.
- Check the book for errors and story issues.
- Hire an illustrator to design a winning cover and interior artwork.
- Format the book so that it prints correctly.
- Pay for printing the book and all other publishing expenses.
- Release the book digitally, compatible with all readers.
- Promote and publicize the author and the book. These services could be limited.
- Keep track of sales and accounting.
- Make sure the book gets distributed into retail "brick and mortar" or online stores.
- Continue to print and distribute the books to stores.

An author who sells thousands of self-published books has leverage when deciding to approach a literary agent or traditional publisher about a contract. If the author gets very popular by self-publishing, a representative from a traditional publishing

house may come knocking and make a really nice offer to publish the book. These days, so many authors are publishing on their own that big publishers play a waiting game to see which self-published authors rise to the top of the heap.

Even a traditional publishing house expects its authors to **promote** and **publicize** their books by building a website, writing blogs, sending emails, visiting schools, boosting their social media presence, participating in interviews, and so forth.

Nowhere on the planet can authors just sit back and wait for their book to become a bestseller, no matter how the book is published.

If you decide not to self-publish with KDP and want to submit your story to a traditional publishing house, check to see if and how the publisher will accept your artwork. Most publishers like to assign their choice of illustrators to manuscripts. Remember, *The Writer's Market* reference book has contact and submission guidelines for writers. The manuscript review process can take three to twelve months. Editors have stacks and stacks of books to review, with more being delivered every day.

The Traditional Publishing House ADVANCE

How does an established traditional publishing house pay authors and illustrators? Traditional publishing houses pay authors and illustrators an **advance** at the beginning of the publishing process, sometimes in installments. Think of it as the money (royalty) paid "in advance" or before a book goes to print.

It's important to note that Amazon KDP does not pay advances to authors or illustrators.

Most publishers calculate the advance based on how many books they think they will sell in the first six to twelve months after a book is on the market. Average advances run between $1000 and $15,000 per book, but bestselling authors typically get paid more. Books have to sell to earn royalties. Once the advance is paid, it is possible an author will never see a penny more.

Authors who are new to the market do not usually get a huge advance. When J. K. Rowling first published *Harry Potter and the Philosopher's Stone*, she made a deal with a small traditional publisher named Bloomsbury to print 500 copies for a £2,500 advance, which is approximately $3,198 in United States dollars. Obviously, no one would offer her that amount now.

Traditional Publishing House
ROYALTIES

As books sell, traditional publishing houses pay a **royalty**, or a percentage of money stated in the contract, to the author and illustrator for every book sold. If a book sells for $10.00 in the store, and the traditional publisher pays a 10% royalty to the author, then the author earns 10% of $10.00 or $1.00 for every book sold in the store. If an author has been paid a $4,000 advance, then the author will first need to earn $4,000 in royalties (in this case, 4000 books at $1.00 each) from sales of the book to recoup the advance before receiving any additional royalties. As long as the book is still in print and selling, the author continues to receive royalty checks when books are sold.

Why is the royalty such a small percentage? The traditional publishing house is taking all of the risks and responsibilities of costs, time, and manpower to design, edit, print, distribute, ship, and market the book.

Traditional Publishing House
- Book sells retail for $10.00
- Publisher pays 10% royalty
= Author is paid $1.00

Minus the agent's fees.

Well-known athletes, models, actors, actresses, talk show hosts, politicians, social media influencers, and other famous people receive high advances for their books because they are popular enough to attract lots of attention.

It is easier for famous people to promote their books since they already have a large following of fans. Fans want to meet them, so they come to their signings and buy books for autographs. They are also welcome on talk shows and radio shows because of who they are and what they do.

WORK for HIRE

When authors and illustrators are paid a flat fee to write something specific in exchange for ownership or a copyright of their work, it is called **work for hire.** There is no advance, and there are no royalties paid with this kind of employment, so neither the author nor the illustrator benefits if the written work is financially successful. Look at your contract carefully and know what you are getting paid to do. **KDP does not contract works for hire.**

LITERARY AGENTS

Unfortunately, most of the established traditional publishing houses won't read a manuscript if it's not represented by an agent. **Literary agents** have relationships with traditional publishing houses and represent authors and illustrators who want to get published. These agents are "in the know" and can get books reviewed faster than if an author sends the book directly to the publishing house without an agent's representation. If the agent has a good reputation, the publisher respects his or her opinion about the book.

Authors submit a manuscript to a literary agent and wait for an acceptance or a rejection notification, just like they do with a traditional publishing house.

Literary agents have in-depth knowledge of the publishing world. Using an agent or not is like the difference between showing up at a party with an invitation and showing up at a party hoping someone will recognize you and let you in the door. Agents know what publishers are paying authors and illustrators, what publishers are buying, and what is selling in the market. They check to see if stories make sense, if the plot has any holes, if the characters are relatable, and if the writing is refined.

Literary agents don't work for free. They have a vested interest in getting an author's book published and will negotiate the author's contract with the publisher. As a result, an author pays their agent 10% to 15% commission on every book sold.

Literary agents aren't like the agents actors and musicians use. They don't set up promotional tours, book signings, or readings, arrange for radio and television interviews, or coordinate print advertising in newspapers and magazines. That is the job of the author or a publicist. There is also no guarantee the traditional publishing house will provide these services unless they are included in the contract.

If your book continues to be rejected by literary agents and traditional publishing houses, it could be time to take a closer look at your story and/or your writing skills. Review your manuscript! Workshop it! Revise it! Rewrite it! Then, self-publish it.

Publishing the traditional way is a waiting game, so authors who want to follow proper publishing protocols should consider writing three <u>different</u> books.

- One manuscript for soliciting a literary agent
- One manuscript to submit to a traditional publishing house
- One manuscript to self-publish

That way, an author can wait for their body of work to be accepted or rejected by a literary agent and a traditional publishing house, while continuing to move forward with their writing career. A traditional publishing house typically won't be interested in your self-published book unless it becomes popular or fulfills a need for them. **Do not send them a complete printed and bound version** of your book. **You must retain the rights to your work** in order to offer it to a traditional publishing house, so read any publishing contract you enter into carefully. Follow the publisher or agent's submission guidelines.

www.AbridgeClub.com

REJECTION

Rejection in traditional publishing refers to someone not accepting your work, for whatever reason, and not offering to publish your book. It is not personal. **You don't have to worry about Amazon KDP rejecting your self-published book.** They will print almost any book you submit as long as you have followed their guidelines, uploaded the files correctly, and have not stolen someone else's work.

If you choose not to self-publish and decide to submit your manuscript to a traditional publisher who can print your book, your book will either be accepted or rejected. Authors are very familiar with the term "rejection."

Imagine that you send your manuscript to an editor, and the editor doesn't like your book. He or she is a person who has opinions, life experiences, challenges, goals, and ideas that may not align with yours. Rejection is subjective: based on or influenced by personal feelings, tastes, or opinions. If a person had a bad experience in middle school, they might not like stories that center around middle school.

Think of rejection as a garage sale where you are selling your personal treasures. One person will walk right past your prized possession and think it's junk, and another person will stop and say, "I can't believe I found one of these!"

Editors review your manuscript at a traditional publishing house. They may reject your book for a variety of reasons.

- **Your story isn't unique or fresh enough.** The editors have other stories just like yours. Your book doesn't have a clever enough hook or theme that will make it stand out from other books in the marketplace.
- **Your story is missing something.** It could be lacking an apparent conflict, a firm resolution, character development, clarity, or any number of things.
- **The publisher doesn't handle your type of story.** You wrote a mystery, and they publish romances. They publish autobiographies, and you wrote a fairytale.
- **Your story isn't written for the publisher's audience.** They publish board books for babies, and yours is a picture book for preschoolers.
- **Your message is too strong.** Books with obvious morals or lessons can feel preachy. You might have too many lessons, as well.
- **Your book has too much text.** Picture books typically range from 300 to 700 words.
- **Your story doesn't match the picture book format**. It would work better as an early reader or a chapter book.
- **Your story just doesn't "wow" them.**

If traditional publishers reject your story, don't give up. Keep an open mind. Listen to their feedback, take another look at your book, make the necessary adjustments, and either resubmit or self-publish your book and prove them wrong. You may attract their attention by selling an impressive number of books.

Keep in mind that while there are some publishers who can't see past what sold yesterday, there are also authors who are too close-minded to listen to constructive criticism.

Just remember, you can't please EVERYONE. Once your book is published, there will still be critics who leave feedback and reviews that may not be flattering, or even nice.

POPULAR REJECTED BOOKS!

See if you recognize any of these well-known authors and their rejected books.

- ***The Giving Tree,*** by Shel Silverstein
  Shel was told, *"This book will never sell."* It sold over five million copies.

- ***Harry Potter,*** by J. K. Rowling
  This book was rejected over ten times by big publishing houses. It finally sold after one agent's eight-year-old daughter nagged him into taking on the book. It has made over 10 billion dollars in books, movies, toys, collectibles, and theme park experiences.

- ***Wizard of Oz,*** by L. Frank Baum
  This book was rejected so many times that Frank kept a rejection journal called *"A Record of Failure."* It is now one of the best-known American stories, has been translated into multiple languages, and has been adapted into films and musicals.

- ***The Tale of Peter Rabbit,*** by Beatrix Potter
  This book was rejected so many times that Beatrix decided to self-publish 250 copies. It has since sold 45 million copies and been made into a movie.

- ***A Wrinkle in Time***, by Madeleine L'Engle
  Twenty-six publishers rejected this book. It won a 1963 Newbery Medal, became an international best-seller, has sold over 8 million copies, and was made into a movie twice.

- ***The One in the Middle Is the Green Kangaroo,*** by Judy Blume
  Judy's first book was rejected for two years. She tells writers, *"Each time I sent a story or book off to a publisher, I would sit down and begin something new. Don't let anyone discourage you."*

- **Books by Dr. Seuss**
  Dr. Seuss was told that his books were "too *different from other juveniles on the market to warrant its selling.*" He has 300 million in sales and is the 9th best-selling fiction author of all time. It's okay to break the rules.

NOTES

NOTES

NOTES

NOTES

NOTES

NOTES

NOTES

NOTES

NOTES

NOTES

GLOSSARY

Adhesive casebound	Books bound with adhesive and encased in a hardcover. (pg. 60)
Advance	The money paid to the author and illustrator by a traditional publishing house at the beginning of the publishing process, sometimes in installments. (pgs. 11, 100)
Amazon KDP	A fast, free, and full-service for authors to self-publish their books in digital format to a global audience (pgs. 9, 10)
Artwork	The pictures and illustrations in a book. (pgs. 38, 39, 40, 43-47)
Audience	The group of people who would be the most helped or entertained by your book. (pg. 6, 14)
Back (of book)	The thick protective outer part you see when you flip over a book. (pg. 48)
Barcode	A series of printed lines of varying widths that can be read by an optical scanner. (pgs. 48, 62, 78, 80, 82)
Binding	The material that holds the pages of a book together, especially the cover. (pgs. 8, 59)
Blank pages	The unused pages of a book. (pgs. 51, 54, 55)
Bleed	Printing that goes beyond the edge of where the pages are trimmed. (pgs. 47, 58)
Board books	A book for very small children or babies, with the pages pasted to heavy cardboard, making them very thick. (pg. 60)
Bookshelf	The hub of an author's Amazon KDP account, where authors can publish a new book, select a book from self-published inventory, upload content, and order author copies. (pgs. 9, 10, 11, 12)
Border	A narrow strip of color or ornamental design along an edge of a page, text box, or picture. (pg. 58)
Cataloging-in-Publication Data (CIP)	A bibliographic record prepared by the Library of Congress for a book that has not yet been published. (pg. 77)
Characters	A human, animal, being, creature, or object that pushes the story along a plotline. (pg. 17)
CMYK (Colors)	A color model for combining primary pigments. The C stands for cyan (aqua), M stands for magenta (pink), Y for yellow, and K for Key. (pgs. 44, 45, 83)
Coil binding	A method of binding where a single spiraled piece of wire or plastic is wound through holes at the edges of loose-leaf pages. (pg. 60)
Color palette	A range of colors. (pgs. 45, 51)
Color profiles	Color profiles define the colors we capture with our cameras and see on our displays. (pg. 46)
Color spaces	A color space is a useful tool for printers and designers to understand the color capabilities of a device or digital file. (pg. 46)
Color variance	This means that specific colors may look slightly different from the beginning of a run to the end of the run, and differences become more pronounced between different runs. (pg. 45)
Commercial Offset printing	An industrial printing process in which ink is transferred from a plate, usually made of metal, onto a rubber sheet, which is then rolled onto a large sheet of paper that is fed through press. (pgs. 46, 50, 52)
Commercial-free	The use of images to make money or in any sort of "for-profit" or promotional endeavor. (pg. 38)
Content	The subject the writing deals with, the story that the writing tells, or the ideas that the writing expresses. (pg. 73)

Copyeditor	A person who edits a manuscript to find and correct errors in style, punctuation, and grammar. (pg. 29)
Copyright infringement	To use work that is protected by copyright law without permission, such as reproducing, distributing, displaying in public, or performing the protected work - or imitating the work of another person. (pg. 38)
Copyright notice	A notice that identifies who owns the rights to written work, a story, book, etc. (pg. 77)
Copyright page	The second interior page of the book, where important information about the book is printed (pgs. 76-80)
Copyright-free	The right to use copyright material or intellectual property without having to pay for it. (pg. 38)
Cover (of book)	The thick protective outer part on the front that displays the title, an image that will attract a buyer, and the name of the author and illustrator. (pgs. 48, 57)
Description	A short statement or paragraph that explains the subject or topic of a book. (pgs. 48, 74)
Dialog	A conversation between two people. (pg. 22)
Didactic books	A type of book that is designed to teach the reader something; to instruct and entertain. (pg. 24)
Diversity	The inclusion of different types of people. An understanding that each individual is unique. (pg. 19)
E-books	Downloadable books that can be read on devices such as tablets, phones, and computers. (pg. 61)
Edit	To prepare written work to be published or used: make changes, condense, rearrange, correct mistakes, etc. (pg. 37)
Emotion	A state of mind that results from one's circumstances, a mood: happy, sad, mad, embarrassed, depressed, etc. (pgs. 18, 24, 26)
Expanded distribution	Access to a larger audience through more online retailers, bookstores, libraries, academic institutions, and distributors within the United States. (pgs. 9, 50, 63, 81, 88)
Fiction	Stories created from one's imagination. (pg. 14)
Finish	The surface appearance of a manufactured material or object, i.e., glossy or matte. (pg. 49)
First-person POV	Someone is telling the reader his or her story, including thoughts, opinions, emotions, actions, and so on, using "I" or "we." (pg. 28)
First rights	The rights given to a publisher to publish the book first. (pg. 97)
Five senses	The faculties of sight, smell, hearing, taste, and touch. (pg. 23)
Flattening	A process that combines all the layers in artwork into a single background layer. (pgs. 43, 46)
Font	The style of text printed in a book. (pgs. 65, 69, 70)
Formatting	To plan or arrange in a specified form. (pg. 44)
Front matter	The first section of a book; also sometimes called the prelims or preliminary matter. It can include the title page, copyright page, foreword, preface, etc. (pg. 53)
Genre	A particular category of book, like science fiction, thriller, horror, comedy, action and adventure, romance, autobiography, and so on. (pgs. 16, 100)
Glossary	an alphabetical list of terms or words found in text or relating to a specific subject with explanations; a brief dictionary. (pgs. 55, 111-114)
Glossy	In relation to the cover of a book, glossy is the shiny surface. (pg. 49)
Google	A search engine on the internet located at Google.com. (pgs. 28, 38, 73, 81, 89)
Grammar	The set of rules that explains how words change their form and combine with other words in a language. (pg. 29)

Grammarly.com	A free online grammar checker that corrects common grammar errors, spelling mistakes, and detects stylistic elements. See also Scribens.com. (pg. 29)
Gutter (of book)	The inside margins closest to the spine of a book or the blank space between two facing pages in the center of a book. The part that runs down the middle of a spread. (pgs. 47, 48)
Hardcover books	Books with hard, durable covers. (pg. 59)
Illustration	A picture, design, work of art, or diagram. (pgs. 39-43)
Inclusive education	In education, inclusion involves supporting people with disabilities through individual learning goals, accommodations, and modifications. When schools, classrooms, programs, and activities are designed so that all students learn and participate together. (pg. 19)
Interior pages	The set of pages or leaves on the inside of a book. (pgs. 48, 49, 50)
International Standard Book Number (ISBN)	A unique number that is assigned to every book before publication that identifies the details of the book: language, country of origin, and publisher. (pgs. 81, 82)
ISBN	International Standard Book Number (pgs. 81, 82)
KDP	Kindle Direct Publishing, by Amazon. (pg. 9)
Keywords	Keywords are words and short phrases that define the subject of your book. (pgs. 73, 74, 84)
Kindle Kid's Book Creator	A program on KDP that helps authors format a Kindle E-book. (pg. 61)
Landscape	A horizontal page or book orientation in which the long sides of the rectangle are at the top and the bottom, and the short sides are on the left and right sides to resemble a long rectangle. (pg. 63)
Layering	The act of placing one design or part of an illustration over another. (pg. 46)
Layout	The arrangement of text, images, pages, and other objects. (pgs. 52, 54)
Leading	The space between lines of text. (pg. 71)
Leaf (in book)	The page of a book or a sheet of paper in a pile. (pgs. 59, 60)
Library of Congress	The largest library in the United States, with a classification system for every book in the nation. (pg. 77)
Limited-content books	Books with little or no content, such as journals. (Pgs. 9, 81)
Literary agent	A professional agent who acts on behalf of an author in dealing with publishers and others to promote the author's work. (pg. 102)
Logical order	The facts, information, or research are reasonably or sensibly organized in a way that something would happen, or in a way that makes sense. (pg. 39)
Low-content books	Books with little or no content. (pgs. 9, 81)
Main character	A person or other being who is the major focus of the story, has a major role in the plot, and/or interacts regularly with main characters. (pgs. 17, 19)
Manuscript	An original book, document, or piece of music written by hand or typed that has not been published. (pgs. 25, 61)
Margins	The areas immediately adjacent to the edges of each page that protect text and illustration from running off the page and being cut off during the manufacturing process. (pg. 47)
Matte	In relation to the cover of a book, a surface that is dull and flat with no shine. (pg. 49)
Medium	The material or form used by an artist, composer, or writer, such as pen and ink, watercolor, acrylic paint, pastel chalk, etc. (pg. 39)
Near rhyme	Rhyming in which the words sound the same but do not rhyme perfectly. (pg. 30)
Niche market	A group of potential buyers who share an interest in specific product features or services. (pg. 89)
Nonfiction	A story or writing that is based on fact. (pgs. 14, 23, 24)
Orientation	The physical position or direction of something. i.e., portrait (tall and thin) vs. landscape (long and wide). (pg. 63)
Page count	The number of pages in the interior of a book. (pg. 53)

Pagination	Indication of the sequence of pages in (a book, manuscript, etc.) by placing numbers or other characters on each leaf/page. Picture books don't typically have page numbers.
Paper color	The color of the paper inside of the book. (pg. 50)
Paper weight	The weight of the paper or thickness of the paper stock used to make a book. (pg. 50)
Paperback books	Books with covers that are printed on cover stock, or heavyweight paper. (pg. 59)
Perfect binding	A method of binding loose-leaf pages where the pages and cover are glued together at the spine. (pg. 59)
Perspective	A way of looking at or thinking about something. The way readers see and experience the events and feelings in the story. (pg. 41)
Picture book	A book containing many illustrations that is especially for children. (pg. 5)
Plagiarism	The practice of taking someone else's work or ideas and passing them off as one's own. (pg. 27)
Plot	The storyline of the text or the main events of the story written in sequence. (pg. 17)
Point of view (POV)	The opinions or feelings of a person involved in your story. (pgs. 28, 29)
Portrait	A vertical page or book orientation in which the long sides of the rectangle are on the left and right sides, and the short sides of the rectangle are on the top and bottom. (pg. 63)
Pre-assigned Control Number (PCN)	The number assigned to each book in the Library of Congress. (pg. 77)
Print run	The number of copies of a book, magazine, pamphlet, etc. that is printed at one time. (pgs. 50, 62, 78)
Print-on-demand	A way of digitally printing books only as you need them, or after they are purchased. (pg. 8)
Promote	To actively support an author and further the progress and sales of a book. (pgs. 78, 91-92)
Proofreader	A person who finds and corrects mistakes in a story before the final copies are printed. (pgs. 29, 84)
Public domain	Creative material that is free for public use and is not protected by intellectual property laws such as copyright, trademark, or patent laws. (pg. 38)
Publication date	The date a book is published and made available to the public. (pg. 86)
Publicize	To make a person or something widely known. (pgs. 89, 99)
Purpose of a story	The most important thing a reader is supposed to walk away with, like new information, a lesson, or a moral of the story. (pg. 26)
Rejection	The act of refusing to accept a file or upload (pg. 86). Or, a traditional publisher refusing to buy a book. (pg. 102)
Reporting	Giving a spoken or written account of something that one has observed, heard, done, or investigated. (pg. 18)
Resolution	refers to the clarity and crispness of an image, which is measured in points or pixels per metric unit (inch, centimeter, etc.). (pgs. 38, 44)
Retail price	The total price charged for a product sold to a customer, which includes what the item cost to make and the money made from the sale. (pgs. 12, 13)
RGB (Colors)	RGB stands for "Red, Green, Blue." It refers to the three hues of light that can mix together to form any color. (pgs. 44, 45)
Rhyming	When a word, syllable, or end of a line has the same sound as another. (pg. 30)
Royalty	A percentage of money paid to the author and illustrator for books sold. (pg. 11)
Saddle-stitch	A method of binding loose-leaf pages of a paperback book using staples down the middle or the gutter. (pg. 59)
Scribens.com	A free online grammar checker that corrects common grammar errors, spelling mistakes, and detects stylistic elements. See also Grammarly.com. (pg. 29)
Second-person POV	The reader is invited to participate in the story and learns page by page what happens as a result of his or her actions. [Use of "You"] (pg. 28)

Self-publishing	Publishing a book independently and at your own expense. (pgs. 7, 10)
Setting	The place or type of surroundings where the story takes place. (pg. 21)
Spine (of book)	The outside edge where the pages are gathered and bound. (pgs. 47, 49)
Spot colors	Colors generated from ink chosen from a color system, such as the Pantone Matching System. (pg. 46)
Spread	A general description for a pair of facing pages, typically the left- and right-hand pages. (pgs. 47, 49, 57)
Stereotype	An idea about how people will act based on the group to which they belong. (pg. 20)
Story map	A diagram that helps writers organize their thoughts by filling in the elements of a book or story, and identifying the story characters, plot, setting, problem, and solution. (pgs. 32-36)
Storyboard	A sequence of sketches that show the significant changes of setting, dialogue, action, and scenes in a book. (pgs. 39, 52, 92-96)
Submission	The act of sending, or submitting, a completed manuscript to a traditional publishing editor or publication to be reviewed and considered for purchase and publishing. (pgs. 99, 100)
Subtitle	A phrase that follows a book title to give it more meaning or detail. (pg. 73)
Supporting characters	People or beings that are not the main focus of the story but contribute to the story in a significant way. (pg. 19)
Table of Contents	A list of the chapters, sections, or subjects given at the front of a book or periodical. (pg. 52)
Text	The original words and form of a written or printed work. (pg. 25)
Text box	A section or object on a page that allows a user to enter text (pg. 46)
Text color	The color of the font in a book (pg. 71)
Text placement	Where the text is placed in the book. (pg. 72)
Text size	The height and width of text. (pg. 71)
Textless picture books	An illustrated picture book with no words—no written story. The illustration provides visual cues. (pg. 5)
Thesaurus	A book that lists words in groups of synonyms and related concepts. (pgs. 23, 28)
Theme	The main idea or topic of a story. (pg. 15)
Third-person POV	The readers feel like someone is holding a camera and filming the events, or like they are listening to people gossip. [Use of "he," "she," "it," they"] (pg. 29)
Thumbnail	A small image representation of a larger image. (pg. 48)
Title	The title is a name or phrase that identifies or describes a book. (pgs. 73)
Title page	The first interior page of the book, announcing the title, subtitle, author, illustrator, and publisher of the book. (pgs. 52, 76)
Traditional publishing house	A professional company that specializes in publishing books. (pgs. 97-100)
Trim size	The final size of a printed page after excess edges have been cut off. (pgs. 58, 62, 63)
Typeface such	A family of fonts of a particular design. For example, the ARIAL font can be in typefaces as regular, bold, italic, or condensed. (pg. 70)
Unsolicited	A manuscript that is submitted to a publisher without an agent (pg. 97)
Upload	The process of publishing content on the Internet. (pgs. 57, 84-88)
Watermark	A digital design (logo, text, pattern) placed on the cover, page, or image that makes it difficult to copy. (pgs. 55, 56, 74, 88)
Word count	The total number of words in a book, from the beginning of the story to the end. (pg. 27)